Detroit Studies in Music Bibliography, No. 72

Editors
J. Bunker and Marilyn S. Clark
University of Kansas

Isaac Albéniz

Chronological List and
Thematic Catalog of His Piano Works

by Pola Baytelman

HARMONIE PARK PRESS   MICHIGAN   1993

Copyright © 1993 by Harmonie Park Press

Printed and bound in the United States of America
Published by
Harmonie Park Press
23630 Pinewood
Warren, Michigan 48091

Editor, J. Bunker Clark
Book design, Elaine J. Gorzelski
Typographer, Colleen McRorie

Library of Congress Cataloging in Publication Data

Baytelman, Pola, 1946-
    Isaac Albéniz: chronological list and thematic catalog of his
piano works / by Pola Baytelman.
        p.   c.m. — (Detroit studies in music bibliography ; no. 72)
    Includes bibliographical references and index.
    ISBN 0-89990-067-4
    1. Albéniz, Isaac, 1860-1909—Thematic catalogs.   2. Albéniz,
Isaac, 1860-1909.   Piano music.   3. Piano music—Thematic catalogs.
I. Title   II. Series.
ML134.A45A12   1993
016.786′092—dc20   93-35580

With love to
my husband Ricardo
and my children
Pamela and Rodrigo

Contents

Illustrations

ACKNOWLEDGMENTS

I would like to thank individually a few of the many people who played a significant role in the development of this work. Michael Tusa, who was the first to suggest that I should publish this book and who critically reviewed the material. Walter A. Clark, for his generous spirit and valuable comments and suggestions on the section about Albéniz's life. Carlos José Gosálves Lara, music librarian at the Biblioteca Nacional in Madrid, for making available valuable information on Spanish editions and answering many urgent phone calls. My deep appreciation to Skidmore College for its continued support of my work, and for the research grant that allowed me to make a crucial trip to Spain. I am particularly indebted to my colleagues Charles M. Joseph and Thomas A. Denny for their confidence, encouragement, and unwavering support of this project. I also wish to express my gratitude to Rosina Moya Albéniz, granddaughter of the composer, for her assistance and warm hospitality, and to John Danison for his infinite patience and for sharing his unmatched knowledge about computer programs with me.

Particular recognition is also due to several libraries for their help in gathering information, for granting permission to use restricted materials in their collections, and especially for mailing documents requested in many pressing letters: Biblioteca del Orfeó Català, Biblioteca de Catalunya, Museo de la Música (all three in Barcelona), Biblioteca Nacional in Madrid, Skidmore College Library, New York Public Library, and the British Library. My deep gratitude also to the Fundación Isaac Albéniz and to Unión Musical Española Editores for making available much important information and published materials.

I would also like to extend my appreciation to the staff of Harmonie Park Press for their careful preparation of this volume, and in particular to J. Bunker Clark for his professional assistance in preparing the manuscript for publication. Finally, especially heartfelt thanks to my husband Ricardo Dobry, for his constant encouragement, enthusiasm, and advice.

PART 1 ISAAC ALBÉNIZ

INTRODUCTION

The Spanish composer Isaac Albéniz had a distinguished career spanning about twenty-five years at the turn of the century. Albéniz's fame is based mainly on one composition for piano, his masterpiece *Iberia*, which was finished shortly before he died. But the miracle of *Iberia* did not happen all of a sudden. There are about 80 extant compositions by Albéniz (including songs, orchestral and stage works, in addition to those for piano), most of which were successful during his lifetime and are nearly unknown today.[1] The main body of this work is dedicated to a thematic catalog of Albéniz's piano works. The present introduction serves to place Albéniz's works in historical perspective. There is a brief discussion of keyboard music in Spain prior to Albéniz and a short biography of the composer. The introduction also provides a brief outline of the three stages of stylistic development of Albéniz's creative life.

Keyboard Music in Spain Prior to Albéniz

Although Spain has had a long and rich musical tradition, it has generally not been geared towards the harpsichord or the piano. There is no evidence of any keyboard music printed in Spain during the first part of the 18th century.[2] However, some outstanding keyboard works were written in the second half of the 18th century by Father Antonio Soler, Father Rafael Anglés, and Mateo Albéniz. They typically wrote one-movement sonatas in the style of Domenico Scarlatti. The Italian-born Scarlatti (1685-1757) lived in the Iberian Peninsula from 1720, where he composed over 500 harpsichord sonatas and influenced generations of Spanish keyboard composers. Then, in the early 19th century, the cultivation of art music in Spain became stagnant. Italian rather than Spanish composers dominated the musical scene, and opera was by far the most popular genre at the expense of instrumental music. A few Spanish musicians wrote salon pieces and fantasias on operatic themes, but they did not produce any significant work for the keyboard. Starting in the last decades of the 19th century, everything changed. Isaac Albéniz and Enrique Granados—prompted by pioneers of Spanish nationalism like Felipe Pedrell—led the way to a dramatic renaissance of Spanish keyboard music.[3] This rebirth of the Spanish piano literature, which had begun with Albéniz and Granados, continued with Falla, Turina, and Mompou in the 20th century.

---

[1] Antonio Iglesias, *Isaac Albéniz: Su obra para piano* (Madrid: Editorial Alpuerto, 1987), 9. Iglesias indicates that Albéniz himself told Enrique Granados, shortly before he died, that he had written 422 works. However, it is not possible to know how accurate this number is, even though it was given by Albéniz himself. Many commentators of the time indicate that Albéniz was often confused about the titles and the number of compositions he had written. Estimates made by Albéniz scholars range between 200 and 700. There are fifty extant works for piano. A comprehensive list of Albéniz's works is in preparation by Jacinto Torres Mulas in Madrid. The title of this publication will be *Catálogo sistemático de las obras de Isaac Albéniz*.

[2] John Gillespie, *Five Centuries of Keyboard Music* (Belmont, Cal.: Wadsworth, 1965; reprint, New York: Dover, 1972), 109.

[3] Linton E. Powell, *A History of Spanish Piano Music* (Bloomington: Indiana University Press, 1980), 49.

Isaac Albéniz: Life

Albéniz's biography reads like an adventure story[4] (see Appendix B, Chronological Outline). He was a child prodigy and his teenage years were highly unusual, especially by 19th-century standards, with travels not just within Europe but also overseas. It is unfortunate that a great deal of the available information published about Albéniz's life has been based on material from a first biography written by Antonio Guerra y Alarcón and other secondary sources. Guerra y Alarcón's biography of Albéniz dates from 1886 (when Albéniz was 26 years old), and it was based on an interview that the already very successful pianist and composer gave to Guerra y Alarcón in Spain.[5] Although this biography contains some useful information, and it is cited by all important works on the composer, including Collet, Laplane, and others,[6] it also has many errors.[7] There are numerous problems with dates as well as inconsistencies between the information published in this first biography and the data coming from established institutions where Albéniz studied in Europe during his youth. There are also discrepancies between Guerra y Alarcón's biography and another published interview that Albéniz himself gave five years later in London. These discrepancies have been pointed out recently in the outstanding research of Walter Clark.[8]

Isaac Albéniz was born on 29 May 1860 in Camprodón, the Catalan province of Gerona in northern Spain. He gave his first public recital at the age of four, and published his first composition, *Marcha Militar*, when he was eight years old. At ten, he was enrolled at the Escuela Nacional de Música y Declamación (present-day Real Conservatorio de Madrid), and was acclaimed as Spain's greatest prodigy, often being compared to Mozart. Albéniz then rebelled, and by age thirteen he seemingly had run away from home a few times. It is often related that on his last escape, Albéniz stowed away in a ship bound to Argentina, and when found, his fee was paid by the other passengers. There are several versions and a great deal of controversy about what happened next. It seems that after a period of great hardship, Albéniz began to support himself by playing in cafés and every place he could, until he met some influential fellow Spaniards who helped him organize a series of concerts that took him from Buenos Aires to Uruguay and Brazil. Apparently the tour was successful; however, Albéniz became ill with yellow fever and returned to Spain.[9] It is unfortunate that there is no documented evidence of Albéniz's trip to South America other than what he related to friends and in interviews. Albéniz kept a detailed diary during his youth, but there are some gaps in it and there is no mention of a trip to South America.

---

[4] Important Albéniz's biographers are Gabriel Laplane, Henry Collet, and Miguel Raux Deledicque. The chapter on Albéniz's life in Paul B. Mast's Ph.D. dissertation "Style and Structure in 'Iberia' by Isaac Albéniz" contains a thorough compilation of already published information about Albéniz's life, unfortunately not all accurate. Raux Deledicque based his writing, to a great extent, on Albéniz's diaries and published materials of the local press (see below). A new biography in preparation by Walter Aaron Clark is scheduled to be published by Oxford University Press. Clark's brilliant articles on Albéniz's life and his relationship with Francis Money-Coutts have done much to illuminate and clarify a subject that has been often misinterpreted in the literature (see Bibliography).

[5] Antonio Guerra y Alarcón, *Isaac Albéniz: Notas crítico-biográficas de tan eminente pianista* (Madrid: Escuela tipográfica del hospicio, 1886). Although this publication is no longer available, a reprint has been published (Madrid: Fundación Isaac Albéniz, 1990). A condensed version appeared in *Celebridades musicales*, ed. Arteaga y Pereira (Barcelona: Centro Editorial Artístico, 1886).

[6] Much of the information contained in these books comes from secondary sources and it is significantly different in each publication one reads. As Walter Clark suggests (see below), although some primary sources that relate to Albéniz's youth may have been lost, a clear chronology of events should be established based on reliable primary sources.

[7] Miguel Raux Deledicque, *Albéniz: Su vida inquieta y ardorosa* (Buenos Aires: Ediciones Peuser, 1950), 176.

[8] Walter Aaron Clark, "Albéniz in Leipzig and Brussels: New Data from Conservatory Records," *Inter-American Music Review* 11 (Fall-Winter 1990): 113-16.

[9] Raux Deledicque, 126-42.

Approximately at the age of fourteen he began to study seriously with José Tragó and also started touring Spain again, giving concerts in Avilés, Salamanca, Valencia, Barcelona, and other cities. His success was truly impressive and he was widely acclaimed by the press, particularly in Barcelona. Throughout Spain, people talked about the "child Albéniz" as the new Mozart.

In 1875, Albéniz left for Puerto Rico and Cuba in a well documented tour that was met with much success. From Cuba he presumably went to the United States (again there is no documented evidence of this trip), where he seems to have barely survived, returning then to Spain.

Albéniz, fifteen years old, decided to continue his musical education, and in May 1876 he enrolled at the Leipzig Conservatory. Most biographies say that Albéniz stayed in Leipzig for nine months and studied there with Carl Reinecke, among others. However, Clark's recent research clearly indicates that Albéniz stayed in the Leipzig school for less than two months. While there, he studied piano with Louis Maas, theory and composition with Carl Piutti, and also briefly with Salomon Jadassohn. Reinecke, however, was not one of his teachers. Clark states that the reason for Albéniz's early departure from Leipzig to Spain may have been the composer's difficulties with the German language, an explanation that is supported by one of Albéniz's own teachers at the Leipzig school.[10]

In September 1876, only three months after his return from Leipzig, Albéniz left Spain for the Conservatoire Royal in Brussels. It was in Brussels where Albéniz was to have the longest period of formal instruction, about three years. While there he studied harmony, solfège, and piano. In 1879 he won first prize in a piano competition in Louis Brassin's performance class, and left Brussels in September of that year. Then, the following year, Albéniz presumably travelled to Budapest to receive lessons from Franz Liszt. There are many conflicting versions on how long Albéniz studied with Liszt. Clark even questions whether a meeting between the two composers ever took place.[11] Most sources give a period as a Liszt disciple that ranges from six months to two years, and indicate that Albéniz followed Liszt from Budapest to Rome and Weimar.[12] Nevertheless, entries in Albéniz's own diary, quoted by the Argentinian musicologist Miguel Raux Deledicque, state that Albéniz stayed in Budapest a total of just seven days and saw Liszt only once, 18 August 1880. Liszt then had to leave Budapest for Rome, and Albéniz returned to Madrid after a visit to Vienna and other cities.[13] The two musicians never saw each other again. However, although the personal relation between the two composers was indeed extremely short (or perhaps even nonexistent), Albéniz was familiar with Liszt's music and performed many of his pieces. There is no question about the major influence of Liszt on Albéniz's music.

In 1883, at age 23, Albéniz married Rosina Jordana and settled down in Barcelona. He began to study composition with Felipe Pedrell, a musicologist, composer, and the father of the nationalist movement in Spanish music. Pedrell was a crucial figure in Albéniz's life. Under his influence, Albéniz began to incorporate, consistently and systematically, elements from Spanish folk music into his works.

---

[10] Clark, 114.

[11] Clark, 114.

[12] *The New Grove Dictionary of Music and Musicians* (1980), s.v. "Albéniz, Isaac," by Tomas Marco.

[13] Isaac Albéniz, *Impresiones y diarios de viaje*, ed. Enrique Franco (Madrid: Fundación Isaac Albéniz, 1990), 19-25; also quoted in Raux Deledicque, 176-79.

Albéniz lived in Madrid from 1885 to 1889. He taught piano, composed, and performed actively. As a concert pianist his success was such that he was known as the "Spanish Rubinstein."[14] His reviews were consistently impressive, and there are many flattering letters from contemporary musicians praising his playing.[15] His career as a concert pianist reached its peak around 1889, when he toured France, Scotland, England, Belgium, Germany, and Austria.[16]

From 1890 to 1893, Albéniz lived in London and began to devote more time to composition. He became interested in writing for the stage, and wrote some successful songs and operettas. He was engaged as principal conductor and composer at the Prince of Wales Theatre.[17] In 1893 he was offered a permanent position at the Prince of Wales Theatre, but he turned it down and instead moved with his family first to Spain and then to Paris. By this time, Albéniz had made what in most of the literature dealing with Albéniz is called "a profitable contract" with a wealthy English lawyer—Francis B. Money-Coutts—who was also known as a poet and writer.[18] As part of this contract, Albéniz committed himself to set Money-Coutts' librettos to music. Although not all the works resulting from this alliance were as successful as expected, the collaboration was far from being a "Pact of Faust," as it has been called.[19] In fact, it was the financial support provided by Money-Coutts until Albéniz's final days that gave the composer a degree of financial security. According to Albéniz's granddaughter Rosina Moya Albéniz, the composer was able to write his masterpiece *Iberia* because of the continued financial assistance Money-Coutts gave him until the end of his life. Without it, he would have been burdened with teaching duties in order to make a living.[20]

During the years Albéniz was writing stage works, he gradually became active in the musical life of Paris, moving with his family to this city, probably in the late fall of 1894. This rich musical environment had a significant impact upon him and he often attended the concerts of the Société Nationale de Musique (which premièred new works by contemporary composers). Thus he rapidly began to absorb the sophisticated compositional techniques of his French colleagues—particularly of the composers who followed the ideas of César Franck. In 1897, when he was 37 years old, Albéniz was appointed substitute professor of piano at the Schola Cantorum in Paris. His relocation in Paris proved to be a decisive turning point in his development as a composer. As a consequence, Albéniz started seeing his earlier works as too simple, and began to develop a more sophisticated personal idiom. The result was *Iberia*, written between 1905 and 1909. He died in Cambô-les Bains, France, shortly after finishing *Iberia*, after an extended battle with Bright's disease (a kidney disorder) on 18 May 1909. He was eleven days short of his 49th birthday.

Albéniz's personality has been colorfully described by his biographers. He had a keen sense of humor and a great vitality; he was exuberant, kind, and generous. George Jean-Aubry, who knew Albéniz personally, gives the following picture of the man:

---

[14] Henri Collet, *Albéniz et Granados* (Paris: Librairie Felix Alcan, 1926), 47.

[15] José M. Llorens Cisteró, "Notas inéditas sobre el virtuosismo de Isaac Albéniz y su producción pianística," *Anuario musical* 14 (1959): 94-96.

[16] Paul Buck Mast, "Style and Structure in 'Iberia' by Isaac Albéniz" (Ph.D. diss., Eastman School of Music, University of Rochester, 1974), 32.

[17] George Jean-Aubry, "Isaac Albéniz (1860-1909)," *Musical Times* 58 (December 1917): 536.

[18] Rafael Mitjana, "Merlin," *Albéniz y su tiempo* (Madrid: Fundación Isaac Albéniz, 1990), 77.

[19] Mast, 32.

[20] Clark, personal communication.

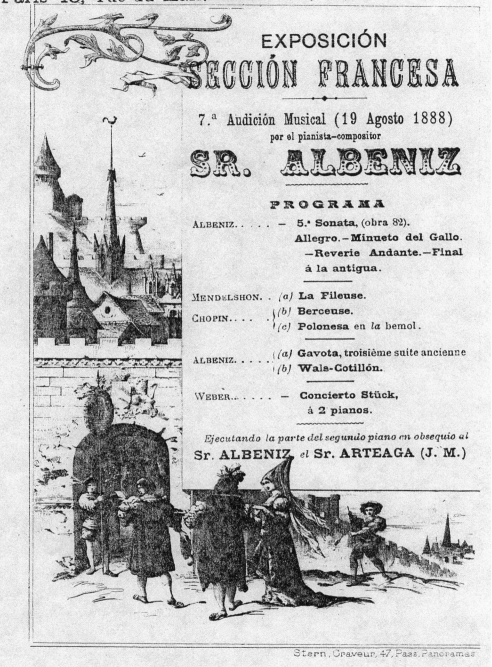

Fig. 1. Program of a piano recital given by Albéniz on 19 August 1888. Printed by permission of the Biblioteca de Catalunya.

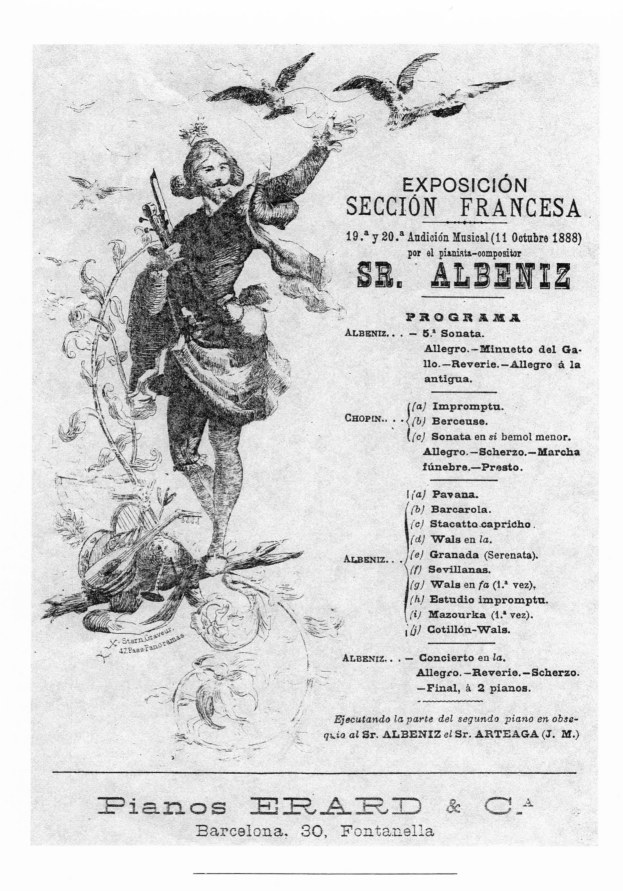

Fig. 2. Program of a piano recital given by Albéniz on 11 October 1888. Printed by permission of the Biblioteca de Catalunya.

I do not think it is possible for any other personality to show such singular harmony between head and heart. His eager intelligence never outran his love for life and things. . . . The kindness of generosity of the man were unsurpassable: I could give a thousand proofs. He was sensitive without wishing it to appear, and the goodness of his heart was a thing of much charm. He was unstinting in his praise of others; his talk was always of friendship, affection, or joy. I never saw him otherwise.[21]

Albéniz left a strong legacy of compositions for the piano, including one of the great works of 20th-century piano literature, *Iberia*. Isaac Albéniz's piano music precisely reflects his personality. It is festive and lush, and it radiates optimism.

Piano Works: Three Stylistic Periods

Throughout Albéniz's career as a composer there is a striking change in the style of his compositions for piano, with three stages of development clearly delineated. From his first simple, short salon pieces influenced by Chopin, Schubert, and Liszt, he moved in the late 1880s towards a Spanish nationalistic style by including elements of Spanish folk music. The third stylistic transformation became apparent around 1896-97 while he was living in France, when professor of piano at the Schola Cantorum. This last style transformation corresponds to the incorporation into his musical language of the more recent and sophisticated innovations in compositional techniques he discovered in Paris.

EARLY WORKS

When he was a young musician, Albéniz made his living by selling his compositions and by giving concerts. In these concerts he frequently included his own pieces. His repertory was unusually broad and covered a wide range of styles from Rameau and Bach to Beethoven, Chopin, and Liszt.[22] This intimate knowledge of keyboard literature left a definite mark on his output of compositions. He wrote at least seven sonatas, three of which are still extant. He also wrote three *Suites anciennes*, which are suites of neo-Baroque dances dating from around 1886.

But the most important influence on Albéniz's early style is that of the Romantic composers. Pieces such as *Barcarola*, op. 23, *Estudio impromptu*, op. 56, and *Mazurkas de salón*, op. 66, are kindred spirits with those of Chopin, Schubert, and Brahms. Overall, these were light works, and their singular charm springs directly from the traditional European salon style of the time. However, they are often superficial and lack a sense of direction and development. Albéniz almost always used the ternary formal plan, and there are numerous literal repetitions of complete sections, as well as reiterations of whole phrases within sections.

This apparent lack of knowledge about structure and Albéniz's difficulty in mastering the processes of development and variation of musical material may be explained by the fact that he really did not have a strong formal training as a composer.[23] He was mostly self-taught, and thus it took him a long time to develop and refine his musical vocabulary.

---

[21] Jean-Aubry, 536.

[22] Gabriel Laplane, *Albéniz: Sa vie, son oeuvre*, préface de Francis Poulenc (Geneva: Editions du Milieu du Monde, 1956), 34.

[23] Joseph de Marliave, "Isaac Albéniz," *Etudes musicales* 6 (1917): 132.

Albéniz's talent for composition was geared throughout his life towards the dance in its many varieties. The set of *Seis pequeños valses*, op. 25, written sometime before 1884, gives us a glimpse into Chopin's strong influence on Albéniz. Each one of these waltzes explores a different mood and has a distinct texture. His choice of key for each waltz suggests a unified tonal conception, beginning and ending in A-flat major, using the dominant E-flat for nos. 2 and 4, and A (Neapolitan) and F major (the 6th degree) for the third and fifth, respectively. Stylistically, they share much in common with all early piano music by Albéniz. A typically optimistic mood prevails, and they have a great deal of charm, though they truly do not rise above a fairly superficial level. There is a great deal of exact thematic repetition and little tonal variety. In only one instance is there a section modulating into a minor key, and at one other point a thematic idea moves from the subdominant major to the subdominant minor for color.

The most interesting waltz of the group is no. 6. There is no redundancy here, and Albéniz is successful in creating a strong sense of expressive and cohesive unity. This waltz was most likely modeled after Chopin's Waltz in A-flat major, op. 64, no. 3. The key is the same, the formal plan is related (though much more concise in the piece by Albéniz), and the curve of the melody in the main theme is also similar, reaching the high C in both cases. Also common to both pieces is the alternation of dominant and tonic bass notes:

Ex. 1a. Albéniz, *Seis pequeños valses*, op. 25, no. 6, meas. 1-9.

Ex. 1b. Chopin, Waltz, op. 64, no. 3, meas. 1-8.

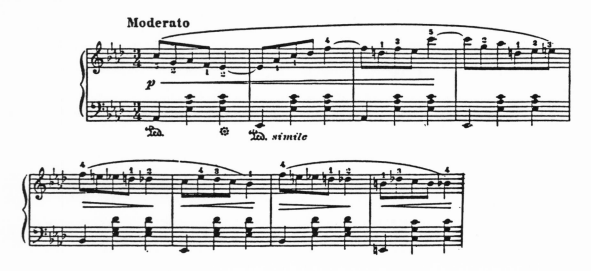

Even the static middle section over a pedal point is alike in the two waltzes, with repetitive rhythmic patterns that recall those of the mazurka:

Ex. 2a. Albéniz, *Seis pequeños valses*, op. 25, no. 6, meas. 25-36.

Ex. 2b. Chopin, Waltz, op. 64, no. 3, meas. 73-81.

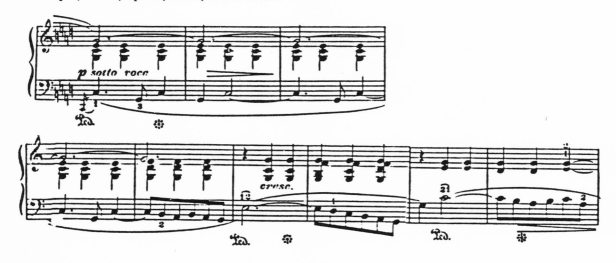

Although Albéniz's waltz does not have the harmonic wealth of Chopin's waltz, nor its refinement, it is quite successful and has much flair.

In his études, Albéniz shows us another facet of his personality. *Deseo* (Desire), op. 40, was written sometime before 1886 and is dedicated to his wife. Its subtitle, "estudio de concierto," was probably inspired by Liszt's own *Études de concert*. Like Liszt's études, it requires a great deal of virtuosity.

Deseo is a rather long, ambitious composition. The introduction opens with a *forte* tritone interval in the bass answered by soft chords in the high register of the piano in a dramatic move quite typical of Liszt. Also Lisztian is the long extension of the dominant harmony so that the tonic chord does not arrive until meas. 15. This passage may have been inspired by Liszt's own *Une Fantasia (quasi sonate) après une lecture du Dante*:

Ex. 3. Albéniz, *Deseo: Estudio de concierto*, op. 40, meas. 1-8.

The constant use of staccato suggests as well the influence of Mendelssohn. The large-scale formal plan is again ternary, and Albéniz uses fast-moving harmonies that give a sense of urgency to the piece. In the middle of the first section, a new lyric thematic idea emerges on the tenor voice, with double notes still moving non-stop in the right hand:

Ex. 4. Albéniz, *Deseo: Estudio de concierto*, op. 40, meas. 49-53.

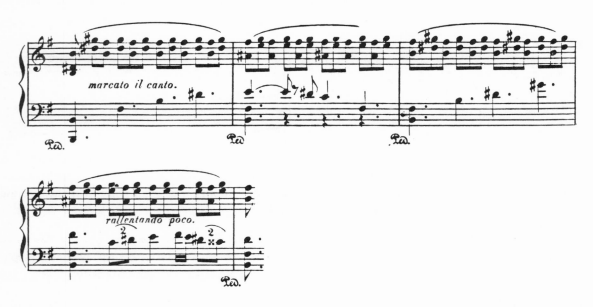

This new theme, significantly transformed, is used later by Albéniz as the main theme of the middle section. The melody is now harmonized and presented over a nocturne-like figuration, thus securing a tight unity of conception for the piece:

Ex. 5. Albéniz, *Deseo: Estudio de concierto*, op. 40, meas. 102-07.

Deseo shows in embryonic form some of the stylistic features that become typical of Albéniz's mature work, particularly in its use of the process of thematic transformation and in the greater cohesiveness of its structure.

BEGINNING OF SPANISH INFLUENCE

Albéniz's second stylistic stage was prompted by his association with Felipe Pedrell (1841-1922), one of the most important figures in Spanish musical history. Pedrell devoted his life to the development of a Spanish school of music. His pupils included the three most outstanding members of the nationalist movement: Albéniz, Manuel de Falla, and Enrique Granados. This trend towards nationalism in music was not restricted to Spain. Nationalist movements had originally begun in Europe as a reaction against the dominant role of German, French, and Italian music. Around 1860, these nationalist movements gained momentum, especially in Russia, Bohemia, and Norway. Given the enormous wealth of folk music in Spain, it is not surprising that in the last decades of the 19th century a nationalist movement burst onto the Spanish musical scene.

Pedrell often expressed the opinion that there was little formal training in the lessons he gave Albéniz, and that Albéniz was not inclined to accept rules and theories.[24] Nevertheless, Albéniz fully absorbed Pedrell's music orientation, and under his influence he began to look for inspiration in the rich Spanish musical tradition. Although this resulted in a significant change in the color of Albéniz's music, the overall thrust of his musical language remained quite simple and unpretentious. He also continued to write works in the European tradition with no marked Spanish character, and his Fourth Sonata, op. 72, and the Fifth Sonata, op. 82, were composed during this same period.

There are four main elements of Spanish music that Albéniz incorporates into his own musical language in this stage:

---

[24] Laplane, 44-45.

1. The dance rhythms of Spain, of which there are a wide variety.

2. The use of *cante hondo*, which means deep or profound song. It is the most serious and moving variety of *flamenco* or Spanish gypsy song, often dealing with themes of death, anguish, or religion.[25]

3. The use of exotic scales also associated with *flamenco* music. The Phrygian mode is the most prominent in Albéniz's music, although he also used the Aeolian and Mixolydian modes as well as the whole-tone scale.[26]

4. The transfer of guitar idioms into piano writing.

Although Albéniz fully absorbed the dance rhythms and musical language of his native land, he never really used actual folk tunes. Instead, he invariably created his own melodies.

Dance rhythms and the influence of flamenco music

Spain is a country well known for its wealth of regional dance rhythms. Although Albéniz was from Cataluña, a province of the northeast, he was inspired most often by the music of the south, particularly Andalusía. The dances he used most commonly are the *fandango* in its many local varieties, the *seguidillas*, and the *bulerías*, which are all southern dances. Only occasionally did he use rhythms of the northern *jota*, a dance from Aragón.

The *fandango* was one of Albéniz's favorite dances. It is in moderate-to-quick triple meter and is danced to the guitar and castanets in alternation with sung *coplas* (stanzas).[27] Among the many varieties of the *fandango* that Albéniz used are the *malagueña*, the *rondeña*, and the *murciana*. Its *copla*, as is usual, derives from *cante hondo*.

One of the most attractive and refined of Albéniz's *malagueñas*, "Rumores de la caleta," is from the set *Recuerdos de viaje* (Travel Impressions), op. 71. It begins with the typical rhythm of *malagueñas*:

Ex. 6. Albéniz, "Rumores de la caleta," from *Recuerdos de viaje*, op. 71, meas. 1-5.

The ascending-descending scale that follows is also characteristic and is present in many of Albéniz's compositions:

---

[25] *New Grove*, s.v. "Flamenco."

[26] Mast, 129.

[27] *New Grove*, s.v. "Fandango."

Ex. 7. Albéniz, "Rumores de la caleta," from *Recuerdos de viaje*, op. 71, meas. 11-13.

Note that the piece—which has the key signature of D minor—begins on the dominant harmony, but in addition the piece also ends on a dominant arpeggio, which is unusual. The reason for this peculiar ending is that Albéniz overlaps a Phrygian scale of A onto the predominant D-minor tonality. On top of this, there is an augmented-second superimposed between the second and third degree of the Phrygian scale, giving an oriental flavor to the dance. The incorporation of the interval of the augmented-second is typical of *flamenco* music, and its origin may be attributed to the strong Arabic influence that exists in Spain. Muslims invaded Spain in 711, and they dominated it during several centuries, leaving an indelible imprint on Spanish culture. Although this augmented-second is quite prominent, Albéniz does not use it melodically—for example in the manner in which Liszt used the gypsy scale. He most commonly uses the unaltered diatonic third degree for scale-like passages and the raised third degree for chordal or arpeggio-like figurations. Paul Mast calls this tendency of the major chord to appear frequently in cadences the "Picardy third" effect.[28]

The *copla* of this *malagueña* is derived from *cante hondo*. As is typical in this type of *flamenco* song, the effective and dramatic use of melodic ornamentation produces an oriental flavor and free-flowing rhythm:

Ex. 8. Albéniz, "Rumores de la caleta," from *Recuerdos de viaje*, op. 71, meas. 26-35.

---

[28] Mast, 131.

Transfer of instrumental guitar idioms to the piano

In addition to dance rhythms, *cante hondo*, and exotic scales, Albéniz also transferred to the piano instrumental idioms typical of the guitar. The guitar is the national instrument of Spain, and Albéniz was by no means the first keyboard composer to allude to it, since the tradition of transferring guitar figurations to the keyboard goes as far back as Scarlatti.

Some alluring examples of guitar idioms in Albéniz's piano music occur in "Asturias, leyenda," from *Suite española*, op. 47, where an hypnotic repeated note alternates with a melodic one in a typical guitar-like figuration, in which the pedal point could be the open string while the other notes are plucked around it:

Ex. 9. Albéniz, "Asturias: Leyenda," from *Suite española*, op. 47, meas. 1-5.

A different guitar effect is created by the use of an arpeggio in alternation with a low bass note, as in "Torre Bermeja," op. 92, no. 12:

Ex. 10. Albéniz, "Torre Bermeja: Serenata," from *Douze Pièces caractéristiques*, op. 92, no. 12, meas. 1-7.

Strumming of guitar chords is suggested in many of his pieces, but most openly so in "Granada: Serenata," from *Suite española*, op. 47, with the repeated rolled chords:

Ex. 11. Albéniz, "Granada: Serenata," from *Suite española*, op. 47, no. 1, meas. 1-16.

MATURE COMPOSITIONS

The final transformation or third stage in Albéniz's style was extraordinary. He moved to Paris around 1894, and soon became active in the city's musical life. He met the leading French composers of the time and frequently attended the concerts of the Société Nationale de Musique, which premièred works of new composers. As a result, Albéniz began to absorb new ideas and incorporate them into his own works. This style change became, at first, noticeable with the rich harmonic vocabulary in *Espagne: Souvenirs* and the complex polyphony of the hauntingly beautiful *La Vega*. These works, from around 1897, mark a transition towards Albéniz's mature style.

Albéniz then began to conceive a complex and ambitious composition that was to have a large architectural plan. The result was his masterpiece *Iberia*, subtitled "twelve new 'impressions' in four books," written between 1905 and 1909. With *Iberia*, Albéniz left behind the simple, transparent style of his youth, and created a highly complex language that uses an elaborate structure and a rich harmonic vocabulary. The fabric of the music becomes intricate, and most striking is the sophistication and amount of rhythmic activity present in each one of the dances of *Iberia*. The writing for the piano is brilliant.

What is remarkable about this rather sudden transformation in style is that Albéniz was able to absorb and integrate the many diverse influences to which he had been exposed during his lifetime. He blended the sophisticated European compositional techniques he learned in Paris with the nationalistic language he developed with Pedrell, and with the virtuoso piano writing he took from Liszt.

Rhythmic complexities

Many facets of *Iberia* are truly extraordinary. Particularly striking are the wealth of colors, the sparkling character of the music, and the complex modulations. But, unquestionably, the most original aspect of *Iberia* has to do with its magnificent rhythms. In *Iberia*, Albéniz is not content to choose a specific dance rhythm for a particular piece. Rather, he combines, mixes, and even opposes conflicting dance rhythms and meters to create an extraordinary palette of sonorities. This wealth of rhythmic activity, including polyrhythms and simultaneous use of duple and ternary meters, is typical of the *flamenco* repertory, and Albéniz found it an invaluable source of material from which to draw.

"El puerto," from book 1, represents a luminous picture of a fishing port seemingly inspired by the Puerto de Santa María in the Bay of Cadiz.[29]   A few commentators attribute the inspiration of his piece to the port of Cadiz itself, and in fact the holograph of "El puerto" that belongs to the collection at the Library of Congress has, at the end, the inscription "Cadix" [*sic*], meaning that perhaps Albéniz originally thought of naming this piece "Cadiz."   Its lively and joyful character is occasionally darkened by the rather nostalgic reminiscences of the *copla*.   The prevalent pattern is 6/8.   From the very first introductory measures, however, syncopations, off-beat accents, and cross rhythms burst forth, painting this Spanish seaport with luminous colors.   By the end of the first sixteen measures, there have been allusions to three dance-rhythms: *zapateado*, *polo*, and *bulerías*. A fourth dance—*seguiriya gitana* or gypsy *seguidilla*—emerges later in the *copla*.[30]

A *zapateado*, danced tapping in rhythm the heels to the floor and the hands to the soles of the shoes, serves as an introduction.[31]

Ex. 12. Albéniz, "El puerto," from *Iberia*, book 1, meas. 1-5.

A motive with the harsh rhythms of the *bulerías* interrupts for only two bars.   The syncopations and hemiola, with a 3/4 time in contrast to the prevalent 6/8 time, is typical of the *bulerías*:

Ex. 13. Albéniz, "El puerto," from *Iberia*, book 1, meas. 6-9.

A few measures later, the main theme of the piece is finally revealed.   Its agitated motion is emphasized by off-beat accents creating irregular rhythmic groupings that help to enhance the lively mood of the piece:

---

[29] Enrique Franco, "La Suite 'Iberia' di Albéniz," *Nuova rivista musicale italiana* 7/1 (January-March 1973): 60.

[30] Iglesias, 232-33.

[31] *Enciclopedia della musica* (1963), s.v. "Zapateado."

Ex. 14. Albéniz, "El puerto," from *Iberia*, book 1, meas. 11-15.

These dance rhythms correspond to the *polo*, a dance with frequent syncopations and a rapid coloratura melody sung to happy texts, often using the characteristic Spanish *olé*.[32] However, before this theme has a chance to finish, the incisive rhythms of the *bulerías* interrupt again with their off-beat accents on the second and fifth beats:

Ex. 15. Albéniz, "El puerto," from *Iberia*, book 1, meas. 17-22.

Many writers refer to the rather nostalgic contrasting section as a *seguiriya gitana* (gypsy *seguidilla*). This particular dance was a courtship dance of proud demeanor, danced slowly and sentimentally. In "El puerto," it is always presented over a pedal point. Even in this calm and expressive passage, syncopations and off-beat accents are abundant:

Ex. 16. Albéniz, "El puerto," from *Iberia*, book 1, meas. 108-15.

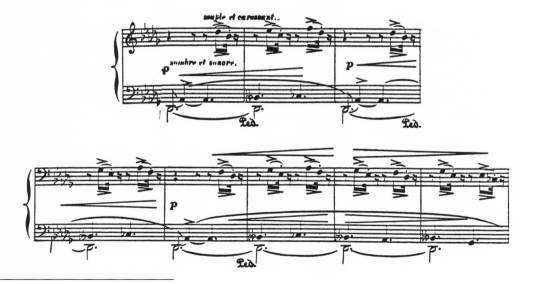

---

[32] *Enciclopedia della musica*, s.v. "Polo."

Texture

Another remarkable characteristic of *Iberia* is the intricate texture of the music. Especially effective in this regard is a section in "Triana," from volume 2. Some commentators see in the structure of "Triana" a free adaptation of sonata form, as it is based on two thematic ideas.[33] Near the end of the piece Albéniz combines contrapuntally the head of the second theme with its own tail, the latter being really a variation of the first theme. The result is a joyful and irresistible passage:

Ex. 17a. Albéniz, "Triana," from *Iberia*, book 2, first theme, meas. 1-5.

Ex. 17b. Albéniz, "Triana," from *Iberia*, book 2, second theme, meas. 51-56.

---

[33] Mast, 273.

Ex. 17c. Albéniz, "Triana," from *Iberia*, book 3, contrapuntal combination of first and second theme, meas. 109-12.

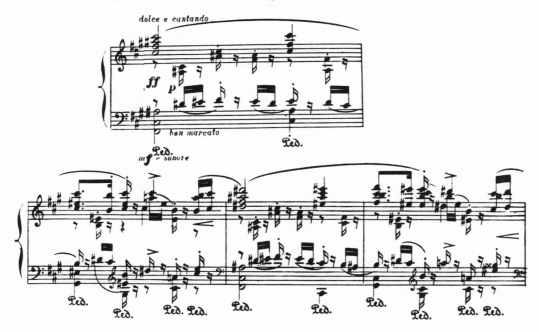

Harmony

Paul Mast, in his dissertation on the style and structure of *Iberia*, states that Albéniz's later works are less chromatic than those of Wagner or Franck, but that he achieves a sophisticated and colorful palette through other kinds of enrichments, particularly modal and whole-tone inflections.[34] Sometimes his harmonic vocabulary can be explained in terms of traditional harmony, but at other times the regular organization of chords in thirds is obscured in favor of emphasis on seconds, sevenths, and fourths, which he calls secundal and quartal sonorities.[35] However, it is the interval of the second that I find most prominent. For example, the emphasis is on seconds in the following passage of "El Albaicín" (even though visually the interval of a fourth seems to be more prominent):

Ex. 18. Albéniz, "El Albaicín," from *Iberia*, book 3, meas. 107-15.

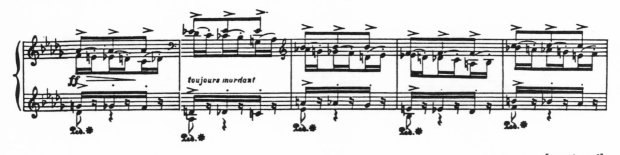

[continued]

---

[34] Mast, 154.

[35] Ibid., 188.

Ex. 18. — [*continued*]

Again seconds are emphasized in the next example:

Ex. 19. Albéniz, "El Albaicín," from *Iberia*, book 3, meas. 297-300.

These sharp harmonic clashes accentuate the strong rhythms of the *bulerías* present in "El Albaicín," and illustrate Albéniz's keen sense of color. Notice the descending cadential figure or tetrachord Eb-Db-Cb-Bb. This tetrachord is typical of much Spanish music and it occurs again and again in *Iberia*. It may appear as a small scale bass line or as a structural design occupying several measures.[36]

Another harmonic device that gives a distinct personal color to the music is Albéniz's use of two superimposed triads. Most commonly, Albéniz gives one harmony to one hand and a different harmony to the other one:

Ex. 20a. Albéniz, "El Albaicín," from *Iberia*, book 3, meas. 263-64.

---

[36] Mast, 165.

Ex. 20b. Albéniz, "El Albaicín," from *Iberia*, book 3, meas. 278-79.

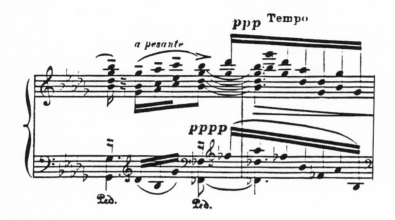

Ex. 20c. Albéniz, "El Albaicín," from *Iberia*, book 3, meas. 250-54.

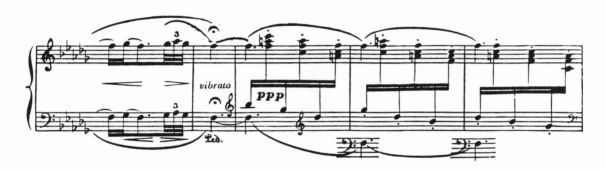

In this last excerpt, the right hand plays an F-major harmony and the left hand overlaps with G-flat major harmony. This effect can be explained as an expanded neighboring tone or, as Paul Mast suggests, an expansion of the Phrygian neighboring tone of the preceding fragment of the *copla*.[37]

These are but a few characteristics of Albéniz's rich harmonic language. Perhaps the best description of the nature of Albéniz's musical thinking comes from Ernest Newman, who wrote the following:

> His music is not self-consciously sophisticated, as that of so many of the modern Frenchmen tends to be; his mind was one of extraordinary subtlety, and his ideas so far removed from the customary ruts, he had to find a corresponding mode of expression . . . no matter how unusual a passage may sound at first, it is always found to talk simple sense when we have become accustomed to it. . . . Albéniz had the real logical faculty in music. He thinks continually and coherently right through his seemingly complicated harmonies, and he has a technique that enables him to say lucidly anything, however remote from the ordinary track, that he may want to say.[38]

---

[37] Mast, 185.

[38] Ernest Newman, "Music and Musicians: Albéniz and His 'Merlin'," *New Witness* 10 (20 December 1917): 495. Also quoted in Carl Van Vetchen, "Isaac Albéniz," *Excavations* (New York: Alfred A. Knopf, 1926), 251-52.

Thematic transformation

The compositional technique at the core of Albéniz's thinking at this stage of his career is that of thematic transformation. This technique, originally championed by Liszt, was widely used in Paris at the end of the century, first by César Franck and then by his disciples at the Schola Cantorum, D'Indy and Chausson in particular. Although Albéniz knew Debussy and heard his music, it is not the more economical and intellectual esthetics of the Impressionist movement that he followed, though there are occasional coloristic moments that have an Impressionist effect. Albéniz was mainly and profoundly influenced by the more traditional group of musicians at the Schola Cantorum. These composers aimed at larger forms, and the techniques of variation and thematic transformation were at the core of their concept of structure.

In "El Albaicín," from the third book of *Iberia*, the *copla* is, as usual, derived from *cante hondo* and is again in Phrygian mode:

Ex. 21. Albéniz, "El Albaicín," from *Iberia*, book 3, meas. 69-81.

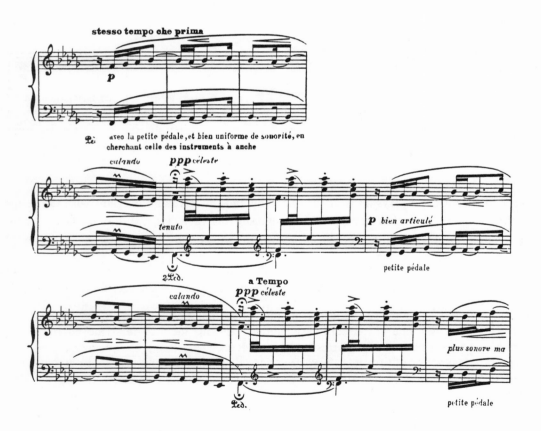

Using thematic transformation, Albéniz completely changes the character and harmonic setting of this simple melodic line to produce a second version, from which he then constructs the central body of the piece. The resulting section becomes a climax of extraordinary intensity. There are dense and complex harmonies underlying this Phrygian melodic line:

Ex. 22. Albéniz, "El Albaicín," from *Iberia*, book 3, meas. 165-72.

Albéniz is not content with simply presenting this new thematic material once or twice. There are actually seven different variations, with the right and left hand taking turns to present the theme, often drifting to distant keys accompanied by complex countermelodies.

In terms of structure, Albéniz, in *Iberia*, moved far from the typical ternary formal plan of his earlier compositions. In "El Albaicín," there is an introduction and a coda, and, in between, four complex sections that use the two basic thematic ideas of the piece: the rhythmic motive of the *bulerías* and the *copla* in Phrygian mode.

Another stunning example of thematic transformation is present in "Fête-Dieu à Séville." The piece begins with a march-like theme evoking a procession going through the narrow streets of Seville:

Ex. 23. Albéniz, "Fête-Dieu à Séville," from *Iberia*, book 1, meas. 1-11.

Typical of the processions in this Andalusian city are the *saetas*, a word that means literally "arrows of song." Toward the center of "Fête-Dieu à Séville," Albéniz inserts a piercing *saeta* in *fortissimo* octaves and long-held chords against a difficult passage in alternating hands. The writing here is in three staves, and Liszt's pianistic influence is apparent. This grand and stirring passage is clearly derived from the simple statement presented at the beginning of the piece:

Ex. 24. Albéniz, "Fête-Dieu à Séville," from *Iberia*, book 1, meas. 99-102.

Much has been said about the technical difficulty and demands that *Iberia* makes on the pianist. The preceding passage is one of many that are well-known for the virtuosity required to perform it. *Iberia* is difficult to read, its crossed rhythms are difficult to execute accurately, and often there are several ideas going on at the same time, most likely at a high speed. Albéniz also has a predilection for overlapping hand positions, where the hands seem to get tangled together at the keyboard.

With *Iberia*, Albéniz wrote his swan song: a true masterpiece of the piano literature. Debussy greatly admired *Iberia*, and wrote the following comment about it in the *Société internationale de musique* (1 December 1913), which has been quoted and translated to several languages:

> Isaac Albéniz, who was first known as an incomparable virtuoso, acquired later a marvellous knowledge of the craft of composition. Although he does not in any way resemble Liszt, he reminds one of him in the generous lavishness of his ideas. He was the first to turn to account the harmonic melancholy, the peculiar humor of his native country (he was a Catalan).

> There are few works of music equal to *El Albaicín* in the third volume of *Iberia*, where one recaptures the fragrance of the blossom-filled nights of Spain. . . . It is like the muffled sound of the guitar sighing in the night, with sudden awakenings and nervous starts. Without actually repeating folk-themes, it is as though this music comes from one who has drunk of them and has absorbed them, to the point of making them pass into his own music so that it is impossible to perceive the line of demarcation.

Eritaña in the fourth book of *Iberia* portrays the joy of dawn, happy to have found a tavern where the wine is cool. An incessantly changing crowd bursts into laughter, laughter scanned by the tinkling of the tambourines. Never has music achieved such diverse, such colorful impression. One's eyes close as if blinded by these vivid images.[39]

---

[39] Quoted in Léon Vallas, *The Theories of Claude Debussy*, transl. Marie O'Brien (London: Oxford University Press, 1929), 162-63.

PART 2 CHRONOLOGICAL LIST AND THEMATIC CATALOG OF HIS PIANO WORKS

THEMATIC CATALOG

A chronological listing of the solo piano works of Albéniz is not a simple task. Albéniz traveled extensively, and many pieces were lost, particularly those from his youth. Therefore, a strict chronological order can only be suggested rather than positively established. Additional problems are encountered because some pieces were published more than once, each time with a different name, and because Albéniz or his publisher occasionally gave the same opus number to two different publications.

The task is further complicated by the many serious misprints and errors made by the publishers, such as including one opus number at the head of a composition and a different one on its title page, as in *Rêves*, op. 201, or giving a composition an altogether inaccurate opus number, as happens in *Les Saisons*, op. 101, which was also published as *Album of Miniatures*, op. 1, by Chappell & Co.

The first catalog of Albéniz's works was the result of the outstanding research done by Gabriel Laplane in 1956.[1] In order to deduce the chronological order of Albéniz's compositions as accurately as possible, Laplane used signed manuscripts (when available), publisher's plate numbers of early compositions, and reported first performances and press reviews of concerts that included Albéniz's works. When no direct evidence was available to estimate the chronological position of a composition, he based his decision on stylistic grounds.

Although the present catalog has been considerably updated compared with Laplane's listing, it certainly does not contain all of Albéniz's piano works, and a complete list probably will never become available. A major contribution of the listing that follows is the inclusion of a thematic index of Albéniz's piano works. This thematic index should help to shed some light on many of the questions created by the confusion in titles and opus numbers.

Much of the original information relevant to the dates of the compositions that was used by Laplane has also been included in this volume. A few works not listed by Laplane have been added, as well as the date and plate number of the first published edition of each work (when available). Some of the confusion about the opus numbers has also been clarified. Titles, as best as possible, are presented in their original language as encountered in the first published edition of each work. Alternate titles used for the same piece are also incorporated, either when translated into a different language, or when a publisher actually gave the piece a totally different name. Different editions for each composition are cited when available, as well as a listing of the main collections of Albéniz's piano works. A few references to textual discrepancies in the editions are also pointed out.

---

[1] Gabriel Laplane, *Albéniz: Sa vie, son oeuvre*, préface de Francis Poulenc (Geneva: Éditions du Milieu du Monde, 1956), 191-206.

There are some early compositions by Albéniz that, although occasionally mentioned by his biographers, have not been included in the main text of the present volume. In those cases no other source of information or score of these pieces has been found, except for these citations. These compositions are listed in Appendix A.

The first known published works by Albéniz were released by Casa Romero and Edición Zozaya, two prestigious publishing houses in Spain at the end of the 19th century. In 1900 both firms were purchased by the emerging Casa Dotesio, which later continued to absorb smaller publishing companies. Around 1904, Casa Dotesio changed its name to Unión Musical Española, which is still a major publisher in Spain.

Prior to this catalog, the dates of the first editions of Albéniz's works written before 1890 were uncertain. The most probable years of publication of these editions were established by the author with the cooperation of Carlos José Gosálvez Lara, music librarian at the Biblioteca Nacional in Madrid. A correlation between the publisher's plate numbers and the dates of these publications that was established by Gosálvez Lara was used for this purpose. This correlation is based in historical references related to the publishers in question, the entries of the musical works into Spain's *Boletín de propiedad intelectual* (Bulletin of Intellectual Property), catalogs from publishers, changes in the address of the publishers, and other relevant information.

ABBREVIATIONS FOR PUBLISHERS

Almagro y Compañía	Barcelona?: Almagro y Compañía
Ashdown	London: E. Ashdown
Ashley	Carlstadt, N.J.: Ashley Publications
Ayné	Barcelona: Juan Ayné
Boston Music	Boston: Boston Music Company
Fischer	New York: Carl Fischer
Calcografía	Madrid: Calcografía de Eslava, Arenal 18
Chappell	London: Chappell and Co.
Dotesio	Madrid, Bilbao: Sociedad Anónima Casa Dotesio
Dover	New York: Dover Publications
Ducci	London: C. Ducci & Co.
Girod	Paris: V. E. Girod
Gráficas	Madrid: Gráficas Reunidas
H. B. Stevens	Boston: H. B. Stevens and Co.
Hofmeister	Leipzig: F. Hofmeister
International	New York: International Music Co.
Kalmus	Melville, N.Y.: Kalmus (Belwin Mills Corp.)
Leduc	Paris: Alphonse Leduc. Editions Musicales
Marks	New York: E. B. Marks Music Corp.
Max Eschig	Paris: Max Eschig
Mutuelle	Paris: Edition Mutuelle
Pitts & Hatzfield	London: Pitts & Hatzfield
Peters	Leipzig: Edition Peters
Pujol	Barcelona: Casa Juan Bautista Pujol
R. Guardia	Barcelona: R. Guardia Ediciones
Ricordi	Milano: G. Ricordi & C. Editori
Romero	Madrid-Bilbao: Casa Romero
Rouart	Paris: Rouart, Lerolle & Cie.
Schirmer	New York: G. Schirmer
S. L. Weber	London: Stanley Lucas Weber and Co.
Universo	Barcelona: Universo Musical
UME	Madrid, Barcelona: Unión Musical Española
Unión Musical Española	Madrid, Barcelona: Unión Musical Española
Unión Musical Española P	Paris: Unión Musical Española
Union Musicale Franco-espagnole	Paris: Union Musicale Franco-espagnole
Salabert	Paris: Edition Salabert
Schott	Mainz: B. Schott's Söhne
Schott L	London: Schott & Co.
Williams	London: Joseph Williams
Zozaya	Madrid: Edición Zozaya

1   Pavana-capricho, op. 12 (E minor)

Date of composition:	1883 or earlier	
First extant edition:	Zozaya, ca. 1885	Plate no: Z. 1198 Z.
Other editions:	Unión Musical Española, 190-?	Reprint of Zozaya, same plate number
	Unión Musical Española P, 1925?	Reprint of Zozaya, same plate number
	Unión Musical Española, 1983	

Comment: Press comment on a performance of this piece by Albéniz in 1883.[2] *Pavana-capricho*, as well as other early compositions by Albéniz, were most likely published by small companies prior to the edition by Zozaya. However, the only extant edition is from Zozaya.

2   Barcarola, op. 23 (D-flat major)

Date of composition:	before 1885	
First extant edition:	Zozaya, ca. 1885	Plate number: Z. 1199 Z.
Other editions:	Unión Musical Española, 1910	Reprint of Zozaya
	Unión Musical Española P, 1925?	
	Unión Musical Franco-espagnole, 1929	
	Salabert	
	Kalmus, 197-?	Albéniz: *Collected Works*, vol. 2
	Ashley, 1979	Albéniz: *Selected Works for Piano Solo*

---

[2] Laplane, 192.

Comment: Printed at the end of the score in early copies of the edition by Zozaya: "Calcog: de S. Santamaría." This means that the edition by Zozaya was probably a reprint of earlier plates done by Calcografía de S. Santamaría.

In the Kalmus and Ashley editions the title is given in French: *Barcarolle catalane* (without opus number). In these editions some repeat signs are eliminated, as well as a whole section at the end of the piece.

3   Seis pequeños valses, op. 25

No. 1 (A-flat major)
No. 2 (E-flat major)
No. 3 (A major)
No. 4 (E-flat major)
No. 5 (F major)
No. 6 (A-flat major)

No. 1

No. 2

No. 3

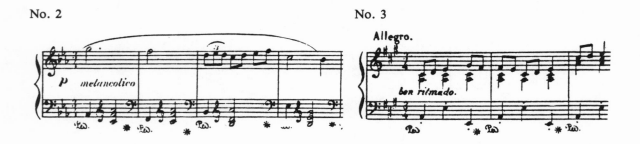

No. 4

No. 5

No. 6

Date of composition:	before 1884	
First edition:	R. Guardia?, 1884	
Other editions:	Zozaya, ca. 1885	Plate number: Z. 1223 Z; dated from about the same time as R. Guardia.
	Unión Musical Española, 1960	Reprint of Zozaya
	Ashley, 1979	Albéniz: *Selected Works for Piano Solo;* title in English: *Six Little Waltzes*

Comment: There is a copy of *Seis pequeños valses*, op. 25, at the library of the Orfeó Català in Barcelona, which has a dedication signed by Albéniz himself to his friend Vidiella, dated "Barcelona, 2 de Julio 1884."

4   1ª [i.e., Primera] **Sonata**, op. 28 (A-flat)

Scherzo (D-flat major)

SCHERZO

Fig. 3. Title-page of *Seis pequeños valses,* op. 25. Printed by permission of the Biblioteca del Orfeó Català.

Fig. 4. Title-page of the "Scherzo" of *1ª Sonata,* op. 28. Printed by permission of the Biblioteca del Orfeó Català.

Date of composition: before 1884

First edition: R. Guardia?, 1884

Other editions: Zozaya, ca. 1885   Plate number: Z. 1224 Z.
Unión Musical Española P, 1925?
Unión Musical Española, 1960   Reissue of Zozaya

Comment: The Scherzo is the only extant movement. There is a copy of this Scherzo at the library of the Orfeó Català in Barcelona, with an inscription written in Albéniz's hand that says "A mi querido, pero muy querido amigo Vidiella; (pese a quién pese) I. Albéniz Barcelona, 6 Octubre 1884" ("To my dear, but very dear friend Vidiella; [whether or not this bothers someone] I. Albéniz Barcelona, 6 October 1884").

5   Serenata árabe (A minor)

Date of composition: before 1886

First edition: Romero, ca. 1886   Plate number: A. R. 6948

Other editions: Unión Musical Española, 1900?   Reprint of Romero
Unión Musical Española, 19-?   Later plate number
Union Musicale Franco-espagnole, 1929
Kalmus, 1970?   Albéniz, *Collected Works*, vol. 1
Ashley, 1979   Albéniz, *Selected Works for Piano Solo*;
title: *Arabe*—the word "Serenata" was
omitted from the title.

6   Deseo: Estudio de concierto, op. 40 (E minor)

Date of composition: between 1883 and 1886

First edition: Romero, ca. 1886   Plate number: A. R. 6955

Other editions: Unión Musical Española, 1900?
Unión Musical Española P, 1925?
Kalmus, n.d.
Salabert

Comment: Deseo is dedicated to Albéniz's wife. Therefore, it was composed after 1883, since Albéniz was married on 23 June 1883.

7   Suite española, op. 47

    No. 1 Granada: Serenata
    No. 2 Cataluña: Curranda
    No. 3 Sevilla: Sevillanas
    No. 4 Cadiz: Canción
    No. 5 Asturias: Leyenda
    No. 6 Aragón: Fantasía
    No. 7 Castillas: Seguidillas
    No. 8 Cuba: Capricho

No. 1 GRANADA: Serenata

No. 2 CATALUÑA: Curranda

No. 3 SEVILLA: Sevillanas

No. 4 CADIZ: Canción

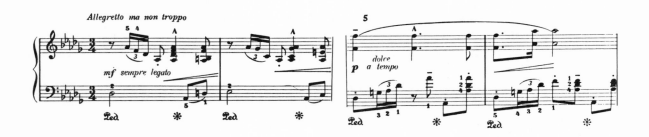

No. 5 ASTURIAS: Leyenda

No. 6 ARAGÓN: Fantasía

No. 7 CASTILLAS: Seguidillas

No. 8 CUBA: Capricho

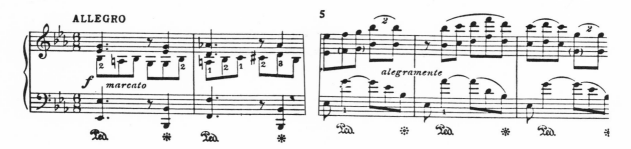

Date of composition:	See information on individual movements beginning the next page.
First edition:	Individual pieces: Zozaya between 1886 and 1901. See also information after the Comment.

Other editions of the complete Suite española:

Hofmeister, 1911	Published separately in 1907, then re-issued with new title page.
Unión Musical Española, 1913	Title: *Suite espagnole No. 1.* The publisher may have added "No. 1" to the title of *Suite española* to distinguish it from Albéniz's later *Suite española No. 2.*
Unión Musical Española, 1918	Revised by Juan Salvat. Title also *Suite espagnole No. 1.*
Salabert, 1929	Most likely a reissue of Unión Musical Española 1918. It is revised by Juan Salvat.
International, 1952	Edited by Isidor Philipp. "Cadiz" is called "Saeta" and the subtitle of "Cuba" is "Nocturno."
Schott, 1960	Edited by Lothar Lechner. Some technical difficulties have been facilitated. Also differences in dynamics with respect to the Unión Musical Española edition.
Chappell, 1960	
Kalmus, n.d.	

Comment: On 21 March 1887, Albéniz put together a collection of pieces to pay homage to the Queen of Spain. This collection included the *Suite española*, with titles of eight dances, corresponding to the present suite. However, at the time, Albéniz only included scores of four pieces: "Granada," "Cataluña," "Sevilla," and "Cuba." The collection did not include the music for the other four movements: "Cadiz," "Asturias," "Aragón," and "Castilla."

It is not known precisely when these last four dances became part of the *Suite española*. When Hofmeister and Unión Musical Española later published the complete suite (1911 and 1913, respectively), it contained all eight pieces: the four original dances, plus four pieces that had already been published as separate works and with different titles. Laplane speculates that the publishers, perhaps finding themselves with an unfinished composition, used pieces Albéniz composed years later to complete it. Since these pieces had different names, the original titles were changed in order to make them conform to Albéniz's original list of movements.[3]

---

[3] Laplane, 150-51.

Whether or not this was done with the authorization of the composer is unknown. In fact, the possibility exists that Albéniz never actually wrote the four pieces he had originally intended to compose. Another interesting fact is that in the 1918 Unión Musical Española edition the four dances that were inserted later into the *Suite española* did not have a dedication, contrary to Albéniz's usual practice. In addition, the plate numbers of each one of these added movements in the Zozaya edition are followed by "bis," meaning that the publisher had printed another composition with that particular plate number.[4]

Individual movements

No. 1 Granada: Serenata (F major)

Date of composition: 1886

First edition: Zozaya, 1886.[5]   Plate number: 1225

Comment: Its plate of publication is earlier than that of No. 2, "Cataluña," a piece for which—according to Laplane—there was a manuscript dated 24 March 1886 (now lost).

No. 2 Cataluña: Curranda (G minor)

Date of composition: 1886

First edition: Zozaya, 20 September 1892   Plate number: 1261

Comment: manuscript dated 24 March 1886.

No. 3 Sevilla: Sevillanas (G major)

Date of composition: before 1886

First edition: Zozaya, 1886   Plate number: 1241

Comment: First performance 24 January 1886.[6]

No. 4 Cadiz: Canción (D-flat major)

Date of composition: ca. 1890 (see Comment for *Serenata española*, op. 181)

First edition: Zozaya, 4 March 1901   Plate number: 1221 bis

Comment: Inserted later into the Suite. Same piece as *Serenata española* op. 181.

No. 5 Asturias: Leyenda (G minor)

Date of composition: ca. 1896

First edition: Zozaya-Unión Musical Española,   Plate number: 1222 bis
                        3 March 1901

Comment: Inserted later into the Suite. Same piece as *Chants d'Espagne*, op. 232, no. 1, "Prélude" (which was published ca. 1896).

---

[4] Laplane, 193.

[5] The dates of the first edition of each piece of the *Suite española* were kindly provided by Unión Musical Española Editores.

[6] Laplane, 193.

No. 6 Aragón: Fantasía (F major)

Date of composition: before 1889

First edition: Zozaya-Unión Musical Española,   Plate number: 1223 bis
3 March 1901

Comment: Inserted later into the Suite. Same piece as *Deux Dances espagnoles*, op. 164, no. 1, "Aragón" (which was published in 1889).

No. 7 Castillas: Seguidillas (F-sharp major)

Date of composition: ca. 1896

First edition: Zozaya-Unión Musical Española,   Plate number: 1262 bis
3 March 1901

Comment: Inserted later into the Suite. Same piece as *Chants d'Espagne*, op. 232, no. 5, "Seguidillas."

No. 8 Cuba: Capricho (E-flat major)

Date of composition: 1886

First edition: Zozaya-Unión Musical Española,   Plate number: Z. 1262 Z.
30 September 1892

Comment: Manuscript dated 25 May 1886. The thematic material used in the eight-measure introduction to "Cuba" is almost identical to that of *Chants d'Espagne*, op. 232, no. 3, "Sous les palmier." See Comment on this piece.

8   Suite ancienne, op. 54

No. 1 Gavota (G minor)
No. 2 Minuetto (A-flat major)

No. 1 GAVOTA

No. 2 MINUETTO

Date of composition: before 1886

First edition: Romero, ca. 1886   Plate number: A. R. 6949-6950

Other editions: Unión Musical Española, ca. 1900   Reprint of Romero edition
Unión Musical Española P, 1925?

Comment: Performed by Albéniz at the Salón Romero on 20 March 1887.[7]

9   Estudio impromptu, op. 56 (B minor)

Date of composition: before 1886

First edition: Romero, ca. 1886   Plate number: A. R. 6951

Other editions: Unión Musical Española, ca. 1900   Reprint of Romero edition
Unión Musical Española P, 1925?
Ashley, 1979   Albéniz: *Selected Works for Piano Solo*

Comment: Performed by a pupil of Albéniz at the Salón Romero on 20 March 1887.[8]

10   Seconde Suite ancienne, op. 64
No. 1 Sarabande (G minor)
No. 2 Chacone (C minor)

No. 1 SARABANDE

---

[7] Laplane, 194.

[8] Ibid.

No. 2 CHACONE

Date of composition: ca. 1886

First edition: Romero, ca. 1886   Plate number: A. R. 6960-6961

Other editions: Unión Musical Española, ca. 1900   Reprint of Romero edition
Unión Musical Española P, 1925?   Title: *Deuxième Suite ancienne*

Comment: Performed by Albéniz at the Salón Romero on 20 March 1887.[9]

11   **Siete estudios en los tonos naturales mayores,** op. 65

     No. 1 (C major)
     No. 2 (G major)
     No. 3 (D major)
     No. 4 (A major)
     No. 5 (E major)
     No. 6 (B major)
     No. 7 (F major)

No. 1

No. 2

---

[9] Laplane.

No. 3

No. 4

No. 5

No. 6

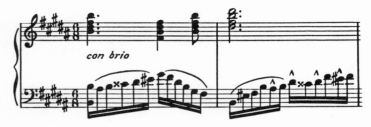

No. 7

Date of composition: ca. 1886

First edition: Romero, ca. 1886   Plate number: A. R. 6964-6970

Other editions: Dotesio, 1900?   Reprint of Romero edition
             Unión Musical Española, 1962

12   **6 Mazurkas de salón**, op. 66

     No. 1 Isabel (A-flat major)
     No. 2 Casilda (F minor)   Same piece as *First Mazurka*, op. 140
     No. 3 Aurora (A major)
     No. 4 Sofía (A-flat major)
     No. 5 Christa (E major)   Same piece as *Second Mazurka*, op. 140
     No. 6 María (G major)

No. 1 ISABEL

No. 2 CASILDA

No. 3 AURORA

No. 4 SOFÍA

No. 5 CHRISTA

No. 6 MARÍA

Date of composition: before 1886

First edition: Romero, ca. 1886   Plate number: A. R. 6975-6980

Other editions: Unión Musical Española, ca. 1900   Reprint of Romero edition

Comment: Two of these pieces, "Casilda" and "Christa," were performed at the Salón Romero on 20 March 1887.[10] (Notice that these are the two mazurkas of the group that were published as op. 140 by S. L. Weber in 1890.) These mazurkas have the same opus number as *Rapsodia cubana*, the following piece. The sequence of the publisher's plate numbers indicates that *Six Mazurkas* was published between *Estudios*, op. 65, and *Rapsodia cubana*, op. 66. Therefore, it was indeed a mistake, either by the publisher or by Albéniz himself, in assigning op. 66 to both works. Unión Musical Española's more recent reprints of the *Six Mazurkas* omit the opus number altogether.

---

[10] Laplane, 195.

13   Rapsodia cubana, op. 66 (G major)

Date of composition:	before 1886	
First edition:	Romero, 1886	Plate number: A. R. 6983
Other editions:	Almagro y Compañía, ca. 1895	Reprint of Romero edition
	Unión Musical Española P, 1925?	
	Kalmus, 1970?	Albéniz, *Collected Works*, vol. 2
	Ashley, 1979	Albéniz, *Selected Works for Piano Solo*

Comment: Same opus number as previous piece. Probably an earlier composition. Performed in an orchestral version at the Salón Romero on 20 March 1887.[11]

14   3ª [i.e., Tercera] Sonata, op. 68 (A-flat major)

Allegretto (A-flat major)
Andante (B-flat minor)
Allegro assai (A-flat major)

---

[11] Laplane, 195.

Date of composition:	before 1886	
First edition:	Romero, ca. 1886	
Other editions:	Unión Musical Española, 190-?	Reprint of earlier publication
	Unión Musical Española, 1960?	Later plate numbers

15   Angustia: Romanza sin palabras (E minor)

Date of composition:	ca. 1886?	
First edition:	Romero, ca. 1886	Plate number: A. R. 6986
Other editions:	Dotesio-Unión Musical Española, 1920?	Reissue of an earlier edition

Comment: There is no precise information about the date of composition of this piece and of the following piece, *3er Minuetto*. Laplane determined their chronological position according to the sequence in the publisher's numbering system.

16   3er [i.e., Tercer] Minuetto (A-flat major)

Date of composition: ca. 1886?

First edition: Romero, ca. 1886   Plate number: A. R. 6998

Other editions: Unión Musical Española, ca. 1920   A reissue of the early Romero edition

Comment: See comment for *Angustia*, the previous piece.

17   Rapsodia española, piano seul, op. 70 (D minor)

Date of composition: ca. 1887

First edition: Romero, 1887

Other editions: Unión Musical Española, 1922
                      Union Musicale Franco-espagnole, 1929   Reprint of Unión Musical Española
                      Unión Musical Española, 1962   Score for piano and orchestra

Comment: Original score for piano and orchestra performed on 20 March 1887.[12] The solo piano version presumably was made by Albéniz, although the earliest score available dates from 1922.

18   Recuerdos de viaje, op. 71

    No. 1 En el mar (A-flat major)
    No. 2 Leyenda: Barcarola (E-flat major)
    No. 3 Alborada (A major)
    No. 4 En la Alhambra (A minor)
    No. 5 Puerta de tierra: Bolero (D major)
    No. 6 Rumores de la Caleta: Malagueña (D minor/A Phrygian)
    No. 7 En la playa (A-flat major)

No. 1 EN EL MAR

---

[12] Laplane, 195.

No. 2 LEYENDA: Barcarola

No. 3 ALBORADA

No. 4 EN LA ALHAMBRA

No. 5 PUERTA DE TIERRA: Bolero

No. 6 RUMORES DE LA CALETA: Malagueña

No. 7 EN LA PLAYA

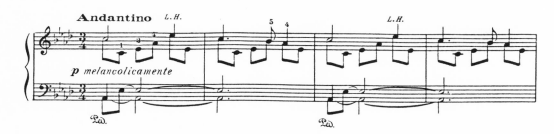

Date of composition: ca. 1886

First edition: Romero, 1886-87   Plate numbers: A. R. 6956, 7001, 7002, 7006, 7022, 7023, 7031

Other editions: Unión Musical Española, ca. 1900   Reprint of earlier Romero edition
                        Union Musicale Franco-espagnole, 1918, 1929
                        International 1957   Edited by Isidor Philipp
                        Kalmus, ca. 1970

Comment: The first piece, "En el mar," was performed on 20 March 1887.[13]

19   Cadiz-gaditana (D minor/A Phrygian)

---

[13] Laplane, 195.

Date of composition:	Probably between 1886 and 1890 (see Comment)	
First edition:	Williams?, 1890?	Plate number: N. 9108.
Other editions:	Kalmus, 1970? Ashley, 1979	Albéniz, *Collected Works*, vol. 2 Albéniz, *Selected Works for Piano Solo*

Comment: The strong influence of Spanish folk music in *Cadiz-gaditana* indicates that it was probably composed after 1886, the year of the earliest pieces of the *Suite española* and of the first works by Albéniz that show the influence of Spanish idioms.

It is interesting to observe that, except for the section of *Cadiz-gaditana* in B-flat major, each one of the other sections in the piece suggests various other compositions written by Albéniz between 1886 and 1890. Specifically, these parallelisms are: a) the guitar-like chords with which the piece begins are similar to those Albéniz used at the beginning of "Granada," from *Suite española*, op. 47 (1886); b) the A-major arpeggio that ends the first section of *Cadiz-gaditana* is almost identical to that used in "Prélude" from *España: Seis hojas de album*, op. 165 (dating from 1890); c) the most striking similarity occurs with "Rumores de la caleta, malagueña" from *Recuerdos de viaje*, op. 71, no. 6 (dating from ca. 1887), in which there are two sections that are almost identical in the two pieces: the scale-like passage of measure 31, and the *copla* that follows.

Because of the similarity of *Cadiz-gaditana* to "Rumores de la caleta: Malagueña," op. 71, *Cadiz-gaditana* has been placed here in the present chronological position. However, its date of composition may range between the years 1886 and 1890.

20   **4ª** [i.e., Cuarta] **Sonata**, op. 72 (A major)
      Allegro (A major)
      Scherzino: Allegro (D major)
      Minuetto: Andantino (G major)
      Rondó: Allegro (A major)

MINUETTO

RONDÓ

Date of composition: before 1887

First edition: Romero, ca. 1887   Plate number: A. R. 7007

Other editions: Unión Musical Española, ca. 1900   Reprint of Romero edition

Comment: "Minuetto" was published by Chappell & Co. as a separate piece entitled "Célèbre Minuet" (1892).

21   3ᵉ [i.e., Troisième] **Suite ancienne**

       No. 1 Minuetto (G minor)
       No. 2 Gavotte (D minor)

No. 1 MINUETTO

No. 2 GAVOTTE

Date of composition: 1886

First edition: Romero, ca. 1887   Plate number: A. R. 7008-9

Other editions: Unión Musical Española, ca. 1900 Reprint of Romero edition
        Unión Musical Española, 1920?   Spelling of the titles changed to
                       "Minueto" and "Gavote"

Comment: Written to serve as a sight-reading test for the position of assistant professor at the Escuela Nacional de Música, November 1886.[14]

22 Menuet (G minor)

Date of composition: before 1887

First edition: Leduc, 1922   Albéniz, *Dix Pièces en un recueil*

Comment: Published after Albéniz's death. According to Laplane, its style is akin to that of *Suites anciennes*.

23 Seis danzas españolas
  No 1 (D major)   Published by Boston Music Co. under
               the title "Habanera" in a collection called
               Spanish Sketchbook (1921)

  No. 2 (B-flat major)
  No. 3 (E-flat major)   Published in Boston Music Co.'s *Spanish
               Sketchbook* under the title "Serenata
               Andaluza"

---

[14] Laplane, 196.

No. 4 (G major)

No. 5 (A-flat major)

No. 6 (D major)

Published in Boston Music Co.'s *Spanish Sketchbook* under the title "Danza" Published by Boston Music Co. under the title "Recuerdo" in *Spanish Sketchbook*

No. 1

No. 2

No. 3

No. 4

No. 5

No. 6

Date of composition: before 1887

First edition: Romero, ca. 1887   Plate numbers: A. R. 7014-7019

Other editions: Dotesio-Unión Musical Española, 1910   Reprint of Romero edition
Union Musicale Franco-espagnole, 1929
Kalmus, n.d.   Title in English: *Six Spanish Dances*
Unión Musical Española, 1980

Comment: Albéniz made a collection of most of the pieces he had written so far, and offered it to "A.S.M. la Reina Regente" (to Her Majesty the Ruling Queen) on 21 March 1887.[15]

24 Cotillon (Carte blanche), vals de salón (E-flat major) or **Champagne vals**

14

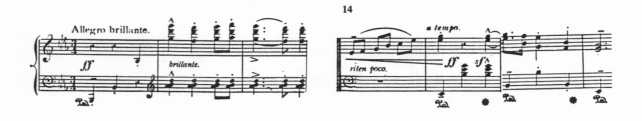

---

[15] Laplane, 196.

Fig. 5. Title-page of *Cotillon (Carte blanche), vals de salón* or *Champagne vals.* Printed by permission of the Biblioteca de Catalunya.

Date of composition:	before 1887
First edition:	Romero, 1887
Other editions:	Dotesio, n.d.
	Williams, ca. 1910
	Unión Musical Española P, 1925
	Salabert
	Ashley, 1979

Plate number: A. R. 7067

Reprint of Romero edition

Albéniz, *Selected Works for Piano Solo.* This piece is published twice in this collection, first as "Champagne Waltz" and then as "Cotillon, Waltz"

Comment: Also known as *Brittania vals*. Laplane indicates that this waltz is the first piece of an album of dances entitled *Cotillon*.[16] In fact, some early scores (as fig. 5) have the following inscription in the title page: "Cotillon, Carte blanche, Album de danses de salon, No. 1, Champagne Wals." This piece is included several times as *Cotillon wals* [sic] in the programs of concerts Albéniz gave during the year 1888. On one occasion, in the concert of 22 September 1888, it is listed as op. 86. No other reference as to opus number has been found. The collection of the programs of 1888 is preserved at the Biblioteca del Orfeó Català in Barcelona.

25   Recuerdos: Mazurka, op. 80 (G-flat major)

Date of composition:	before 1887
First edition:	Ayné, 1887
Other editions:	Williams, 1893
	Unión Musical Española, 1926
	Unión Musical Española, 1962

Plate number: Ayné 23

Title: *1st Mazurka* (no opus number)

26   Mazurka de salón, op. 81 (E-flat major)

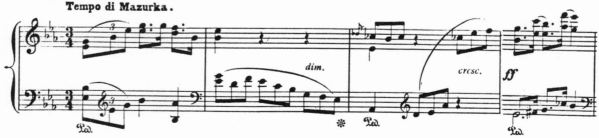

---

16 Laplane, 196.

Date of composition: before 1887

First edition: Ayné, 1887   Plate number: Ayné 23

Other editions: Williams, 1893   Title: *2nd Mazurka* (no opus number)
                     Unión Musical Española, 1962

27   5ª [i.e., Quinta] **Sonata**, op. 82 (G-flat major)

        Allegro non troppo (G-flat major)

        Minuetto del gallo: Allegro assai (C-sharp minor)   Published separately by Unión Musical
                                                       Española

        Reverie et allegro: Andante (D major)

        Allegro (G-flat major)

Date of composition: before 1887

First edition: Romero, ca. 1887   Plate number: A. R. 7085

Other editions: Unión Musical Española, 1900?   Reissue of Romero edition

Comment: Instead of "Allegro," the last movement is listed as "Final à la antigua" in two of the programs of Albéniz's concerts of 1888 (August 19 and October 11).

28   Pavana fácil para manos pequeñas, op. 83 (C minor)

Date of composition: before 1887

First edition: Romero, 1887   Plate number: A. R. 7090

Other editions: Dotesio-Unión Musical Española, 1900?
                      Ricordi, 1973; reprinted 1986   *Il mio primo Albéniz*

Comment: A press review (18 September 1887) of a concert given by Albéniz states that by this date he had already published 83 original pieces for solo piano, without including published works for voice.[17]

29   Douze Pièces caractéristiques pour piano, op. 92
   No. 1 Gavotte (G major)
   No. 2 Minuetto a Sylvia (A major)
   No. 3 Barcarolle: Ciel sans nuage (E-flat major)
   No. 4 Prière (E-flat major)
   No. 5 Conchita: Polka (F major)
   No. 6 Pilar: Valse (A major)
   No. 7 Zambra (G minor)
   No. 8 Pavana (F minor)
   No. 9 Polonesa (E-flat major)
   No. 10 Mazurka (G minor)
   No. 11 Staccato: Capricho (A major)
   No. 12 Torre Bermeja: Serenata (E major)

---

[17] Laplane, 197.

No. 1 GAVOTTE

No. 2 MINUETTO A SYLVIA

No. 3 BARCAROLLE: Ciel sans nuage

No. 4 PRIÈRE

No. 5 CONCHITA: Polka

No. 6 PILAR: Valse

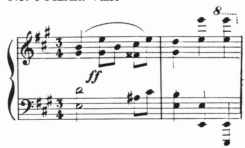

No. 7 ZAMBRA

No. 8 PAVANA

No. 9 POLONESA

No. 10 MAZURKA

No. 11 STACCATO: Capricho

No. 12 TORRE BERMEJA: Serenata

Date of composition:　ca. 1888

First edition:　Romero, ca. 1888

Plate number: A. R. 7113-7124

Other editions:　Dotesio, 1900
Unión Musical Española, 1912
Union Musicale Franco-espagnole, 1912,
1929

Reissue of Romero edition
Title of the collection: *Piezas características*

Comment: The first eleven pieces were played by Albéniz in a concert reviewed by Pedrell on 15 August 1888. No. 12, "Torre Bermeja," was performed by Albéniz on 25 April 1889 at the Salle Erard.[18] The title of no. 4, "Prière," was translated to "Plegaria" in later editions of Unión Musical Española. Some early editions list the first piece as "Gavotte sur un thème de Mlle. Irene Landauer."

30　La fiesta de aldea (E major)

---

[18] Laplane, 197-98.

Date of composition: 1888

First edition: Unión Musical Española, 1973

Comment: Holograph in the Library of Congress. At the end it says: "1er. Tiempo de la Fiesta de Aldea, para Orquesta. Tiana, 22 Agosto 1888." Apparently this is the first movement of an unfinished work for orchestra. Only the solo piano arrangement exists.

31   2 Mazurkas de salón

>   No. 1 Amalia, op. 95 (E-flat major)
>   No. 2 Ricordatti, op. 96 (D minor)

No. 1 AMALIA

No. 2 RICORDATTI

Date of composition: before 1889

First edition: Zozaya, ca. 1889   Plate number: Z. 1335-6 Z.

Other editions: Unión Musical Española, 1920?   Reprint of Zozaya edition

Comment: These two mazurkas, as well as the *Seconde Suite espagnole*, were presumably composed while Albéniz was still living in Spain, before moving to England in 1890.

32   Seconde Suite espagnole, op. 97

>   No. 1 Zaragoza: Capricho (E-flat major)
>   No. 2 Sevilla: Capricho (D major)

No. 1 ZARAGOZA: Capricho

No. 2 SEVILLA: Capricho

Date of composition:	before 1890
First edition:	Romero, ca. 1890 Plate number: A. R. 7161-2
Other editions:	Union Musicale Franco-espagnole, 1929
	Unión Musical Española, ca. 1960

33   Album of Miniatures [Les Saisons], op. 101

     No. 1 Le Printemps (A major)
     No. 2 L'Été (D major)
     No. 3 L'Automne (A minor)
     No. 4 L'Hiver (D minor)

No. 1 LE PRINTEMPS

No. 2 L'ÉTÉ

No. 3 L'AUTOMNE

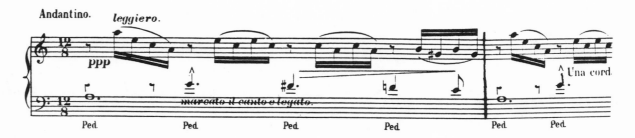

No. 4 L'HIVER

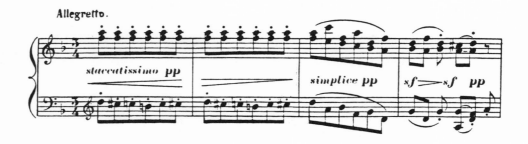

Date of composition: before 1892

First edition: Chappell, 1892   Plate number: 19236

Other editions: Schirmer, 1911   Only "L'Hiver"
                      Girod, n.d.
                      Leduc, 1922   Albéniz, *Dix Pièces, en un recueil*

Comment: Albéniz resided in London from 1890 to 1893 and many of the works written during this period had English publishers.

There is some confusion about a score of *Album of Miniatures* that belongs to the collection of the British Library. This score is published erroneously as op. 1 by Chappell & Co. and, although it is the same composition as the one presently being discussed, it does not have the subtitle "Les Saisons." When the publisher Alphonse Leduc included this set of pieces in its collection (1922), the pieces were scattered throughout the volume, and there was no mention of a collection entitled *Album of Miniatures*. Instead, each piece is under the title "Les Saisons" (with a subtitle corresponding to each season) and the opus number is omitted altogether.

ALBUM OF MINIATURES.

Nº 1...SPRING... | Nº 3...AUTUMN
Nº 2...SUMMER | Nº 4...WINTER

FOR

Pianoforte

Composed by

J. ALBENIZ.

Op.1.

PRICE 3/- NET.

London,
CHAPPELL & Cº 50, NEW BOND STREET, W.
NEW YORK, NOVELLO EWER & Cº

COPYRIGHT 1892 BY CHAPPELL & Cº

Fig. 6. Title-page of *Album of Miniatures*, erroneously published as ''op. 1'' by Chappell & Co.

34   Sonata No. 7, op. 111
      Minuetto (E-flat major)

MINUETTO

Date of composition: before 1890?

First edition: Unión Musical Española?, 1962   Plate number: 19904

Comment: "Minuetto" is the only extant movement.

35   First Mazurka, Second Mazurka, op. 140

First Mazurka (F minor)   Same piece as "Casilda" from *6 Mazurkas de salón*, op. 66

Second Mazurka (E major)   Same piece as "Christa" from *6 Mazurkas de salón*, op. 66

FIRST MAZURKA

SECOND MAZURKA

Date of composition: ca. 1886

First edition: S. L. Weber, 1890   Plate number: S. L. W. & CO. 2825 & 2826

Other editions: Ashdown, 1923   Title of the set: *Deux Mazurkas*, op. 140

Comment: The two available editions of these mazurkas published as op. 140 belong to the collection of the British Library.

36   Deux Dances [*sic*] espagnoles, op. 164

No. 1 Aragón: Jota aragonesa (F major)   Same piece as "Aragón (fantasía)," from *Suite española*, op. 47, no. 6

No. 2 Tango (A minor)

No. 1 ARAGÓN: Jota aragonesa

No. 2 TANGO

Date of composition: before 1889

First edition: M. Eschig/S. L. Weber, 1889

Other editions: Schott, 1921
Leduc, 1922   Albéniz, *Dix Pièces en un recueil*. The title of no. 1 is in French: "Aragonaise, Jota espagnole." Published as separate pieces.

Comment: Also called *Deux Morceaux caractéristiques, Spanish National Songs*.

37   España: Six Feuilles d'album, op. 165

  No. 1 Prélude (D minor/A Phrygian)
  No. 2 Tango (D major)
  No. 3 Malagueña (E minor/B Phrygian)
  No. 4 Serenata (G minor)
  No. 5 Capricho catalán (E-flat major)
  No. 6 Zortzico (E major)

No. 1 PRÉLUDE

No. 2 TANGO

No. 3 MALAGUEÑA

No. 4 SERENATA

No. 5 CAPRICHO CATALÁN

No. 6 ZORTZICO

Date of composition:	1890	
First edition:	Pitts & Hatzfield, 1890	Plate number: 1711-1716
Other editions:	Schott L, 1890-99	Reprinted in 1920
	Schott L, 1928	Revised by L. H. Meyer
	International, 1950	Edited by Isidor Philipp; English title: *España, Six Album Leaves*
	Unión Musical Española, ca. 1960	Spanish title: *España: Seis hojas de album*
	Schott, 1960	Revised by Wilhelm Lutz
	Peters, 1965	German title: *España: 6 Albumstücke für Klavier zu 2 Händen*
	Carl Fischer, n.d.	Revised by Weitzmann
	Dover, 1987	Reprint of Peters, 1965 (includes *Iberia*)

38   L'Automne vals, op. 170

[*continued*]

38   L'Automne vals—[continued]

Date of composition: ca. 1890

First edition: Pujol, 1890

Other editions: S. L. Weber, 1890
                            Unión Musical Española, 1910?
                            Ashley, 1979   Albéniz, *Selected Works for Piano Solo*

Comment: Sectional waltz; each section is in a different key.

39   Serenata española, op. 181 (D-flat major)

Date of composition:	ca. 1890		
First edition:	Pujol?, n.d.		Plate number: 2
Other editions:	Ducci, 1890		Albéniz, *Trois Nouvelles Compositions pour piano*
	Unión Musical Española, 1910?		Title: *Célèbre Sérénade espagnole*
	Union Musicale Franco-espagnole, 1929		Title: *Célèbre Sérénade espagnole*
	Salabert		
	Kalmus, 1970?		Albéniz, *Collected Works*, vol. 2; French title: *Sérénade espagnole*
	Ashley, 1979		Albéniz, *Selected Works for Piano Solo*

Comment: Performed on 14 March 1891 at St. James Hall in London by Albéniz.[19] This is the same piece as *Suite española*, op. 47, no. 4, "Cadiz," and it is often published as *Célèbre Sérénade espagnole*.

40   Rêves, op. 201 (also published as op. 101)
   No. 1 Berceuse (G major)
   No. 2 Scherzino (C major)
   No. 3 Chant d'amour (A major)

No. 1 BERCEUSE

No. 2 SCHERZINO

---

[19] Laplane, 200.

No. 3 CHANT D'AMOUR

Date of composition: ca. 1891

First edition: S. L. Weber?, ca. 1892

Other editions: Girod, n.d.
Leduc, 1922   Albéniz, *Dix Pièces en un recueil*

Comment: *Rêves* has been given three different catalog numbers. Laplane assigns *Rêves* as op. 101 without observing that, if this were the case, *Album of Miniatures* and *Rêves* would have the same opus number. In the edition of *Rêves* published by V. E. Girod, the printed score has "op. 201" engraved with the composer's name. However, the cover page indicates the work is op. 101 (an error that may have created the confusion). When Leduc published *Dix Pièces* in 1922, a collection of compositions by Albéniz, *Rêves* was included also as op. 201 (although the movements are scattered throughout the volume and not presented as a group entitled *Rêves*). Tarazona lists *Rêves* as op. 110 and gives a date of composition of 1891.[20] No. 1, "Berceuse," was performed by Albéniz in London in March 1891.[21]

41   Mallorca: Barcarola, op. 202 (F-sharp minor)

Date of composition: ca. 1891

First edition: Pujol, ca. 1895   Plate number: P. 97. C.

---

[20] Andrés Ruiz Tarazona, *Isaac Albéniz: España soñada* (Madrid: Real Musical Editores, 1975), 56.

[21] Laplane, 199.

Other editions:	Unión Musical Española, ca. 1910	Reprint of Pujol edition
	Union Musicale Franco-espagnole, 1929	
	Salabert, 1929	
	Kalmus, 1970	Albéniz, *Collected Works*, vol. 1

Comment: According to Laplane, *Mallorca*, op. 202, was performed by Albéniz in London during concerts given in the spring of 1891.[22] Original edition in the Biblioteca Nacional, Madrid.

42 Zambra granadina: Danse orientale (D minor)

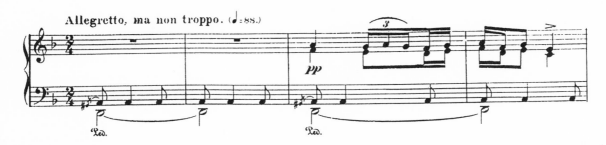

Date of composition:	ca. 1890	
First edition:	Pujol?, ca. 1890	
Other editions:	Ducci, ca. 1890	Albéniz, *Trois Nouvelles Compositions pour piano*
	Unión Musical Española, 1920	
	Williams, 1934	
	Ashley, 1979	Albéniz, *Selected Works for Piano Solo*
	Kalmus, 1970?	Albéniz, *Collected Works*, vol. 1

Comment: According to Laplane, this work and the following piece, *Zortzico*, may be contemporaries of the pieces just preceding since they have a similar style. Also, the fact that *Zambra* is dedicated to Arthur Hervey, an Englishman, could indicate that Albéniz was still living in England when he composed it.

43 Zortzico (E minor)

---

[22] Laplane, 200.

Date of composition: 1891-93?

First edition: Unión Musical Española?, n.d.

Other editions: Unión Musical Española, 1911   Reprinted ca. 1960
Mutuelle, ca. 1911
Boston Music Co., 1914   Edited by C. B. Roepper
Max Eschig, 1930

Comment: See Comment for previous piece.

44   Chants d'Espagne, op. 232

No. 1 Prélude (G minor)   Same piece as *Suite española*, op. 47, no. 5, "Asturias"

No. 2 Orientale (D minor)

No. 3 Sous les palmier: Danse espagnole (E-flat major)   The thematic material used in the introduction is borrowed from *Suite española*, op. 47, no. 8, "Cuba"

No. 4 Córdoba (D minor)

No. 5 Seguidillas (F-sharp major)   Same piece as *Suite española*, op. 47, no. 7, "Castillas"

No. 1 PRÉLUDE

No. 2 ORIENTALE

No. 3 SOUS LES PALMIER: Danse espagnole

No. 4 CÓRDOBA

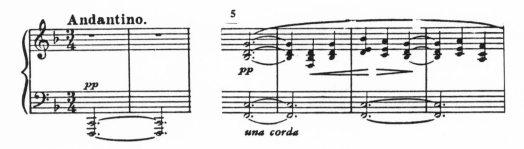

No. 5 SEGUIDILLAS

Date of composition:	ca. 1896	
First edition:	Unión Musical Española, ca. 1896	Plate number: 22
Other editions:	Pujol, 1897	The editor Pujol bought "Córdoba" and "Seguidillas" for 240 pesetas in November 1897, an important amount of money for Albéniz.[23]
	Hofmeister, 19-?	
	Unión Musical Española P, 1925	
	Union Musicale Franco-espagnole, 1929	
	Unión Musical Española, 195-?	Title in Spanish: *Cantos de España*
	International, 1950	Title in Spanish and English (*Airs of Spain*)
	Kalmus, 1970?	Title in English: *Songs of Spain*
	Ashley, 1979	Albéniz, *Selected Works for Piano Solo*
	Salabert, n.d.	

Comment: First works written while Albéniz was living in Paris. See Comment for *Suite española*, op. 47.

45   Espagne: Souvenirs

   No. 1 Prélude (D-flat major)
   No. 2 Asturies (F-sharp minor)

---

[23] Miguel Raux Deledicque, *Albéniz: Su vida inquieta y ardorosa* (Buenos Aires: Ediciones Peuser, 1950), 281.

No. 1 PRÉLUDE

No. 2 ASTURIES

Date of composition: ca. 1897

First edition: Unión Musical Española?, 1897?   Plate number: U. 336 M.

Other editions: Universo, 189-?   Subtitle added: *Oeuvre nouvelle pour le piano*

Unión Musical Española P, 1925?
Kalmus, 1970?   Albéniz, *Collected Works*, vol. 1. Includes only no. 2, "Asturies."

Ashley, 1979   Albéniz, *Selected Works for Piano Solo*. Includes only no. 2, "Asturies," but it is entitled "Espagne."

Comment: The only available edition for no. 1, "Prélude," is that of Unión Musical Española. Unfortunately, its cover page incorrectly indicates the published piece to be *Chants d'Espagne*, although the score included does indeed correspond to *Espagne (Souvenirs)*, no. 1, "Prélude."

46   The Alhambra: Suite pour le piano

No. 1 La Vega (A-flat minor)

Date of composition: 14 February 1897 (Paris)

First edition: Mutuelle, n.d.   Plate number: E. 3143 M.

Other editions: Max Eschig, 1930
                                   Unión Musical Española, 1975   Reprint of Eschig, 1930
                                   Kalmus, 197-?

Comment: Dated manuscript in the Biblioteca de Catalunya, Departament de Música. A poem entitled "Granada" by F. B. Money-Coutts is printed in the score. "La Vega" was meant to be the Introduction to a new suite entitled "Suitte Symphonique *The Alhambra*," left unfinished by the composer.

47   Iberia: 12 nouvelles "impressions" en quatre cahiers

1er. Cahier
   1. Evocación (A-flat minor)
   2. El puerto (D-flat major)
   3. Fête-Dieu à Séville (F-sharp minor)

2e. Cahier
   1. Rondeña (D major)
   2. Almería (G major)
   3. Triana (F-sharp minor)

3e. Cahier
   1. El Albaicín (B-flat minor)
   2. El polo (F minor)
   3. Lavapiés (D-flat major)

4e. Cahier
   1. Málaga (B-flat major)
   2. Jerez (A minor/E Phrygian)
   3. Eritaña (E-flat major)

1er. Cahier

EVOCACIÓN

EL PUERTO

FÊTE-DIEU À SÉVILLE

2e. Cahier

RONDEÑA

ALMERÍA

TRIANA

3e. Cahier

EL ALBAICÍN

EL POLO

LAVAPIÉS

4e. Cahier

MÁLAGA

JEREZ

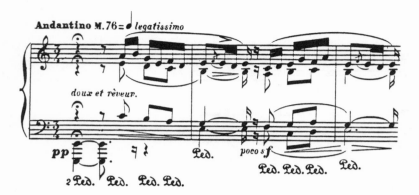

ERITAÑA

Date of composition: between 1905 and 1909

First edition: Mutuelle, 1906-08[24]

Plate number: E. 3083-3086 M. (vol. 1, 1906; vol. 2, 1907; vol. 3, 1907; and vol. 4, 1908)

Other editions:

Unión Musical Española, 1906-09
Gráficas, ca. 1906
Rouart, ca. 1907
Marks, ca. 1909-46

Reprint of Mutuelle edition
Vol. 1 only (miniature score)

Vols. 1 and 2 are ca. 1936 and 1937 respectively; vol. 3 is ca. 1946; vol. 4 is Paris, ca. 1909. Edited by Venato da Campo

International, 1970

Edited by Isidore Philipp; preface by Jean Bowen in all volumes with commentaries about the individual pieces

Kalmus, n.d.
Salabert, n.d.
Dover, 1987

Reprint of Unión Musical Española
Reprint of Edition Mutuelle, including *Espagne: Six Feuilles d'album*, op. 165

---

[24] Notice that the date of the last volume of *Iberia* published by Edition Mutuelle is 1908, which is inconsistent with the date of the autograph of "Jerez," January 1909.

Comment: The editions by Unión Musical Española date approximately from the same years as those published by Edition Mutuelle. Although Laplane gives Unión Musical Española for the first edition, Laura Albéniz (Isaac's daughter) states that Edition Mutuelle was the first to publish *Iberia*. In fact, two of her drawings were used for the title pages of Edition Mutuelle. Furthermore, the early Unión Musical Española editions have the same plate numbers as those of Edition Mutuelle and include the drawings made by Laura Albéniz (which are not present in later Unión Musical Española editions).

There are dated manuscripts for all the pieces of *Iberia* (see each individual piece).

Individual movements

1er. Cahier

1. Evocación (A-flat major)

   Date of composition: 1905

   Comment: Dated autograph: Paris, 9 December 1905. Biblioteca de Catalunya, Departament de Música. Albéniz's title in the autograph for this piece is "Prélude." When and who made the decision to change it to "Evocación" (the final title in the published version) is unknown.

2. El puerto (D-flat major)

   Date of composition: 1905

   Comment: Dated autograph: Paris, 15 December 1905. Holograph at the Library of Congress gives title as "Cadix." Misprint in meas. 131 in all editions—the last note should be a D-flat (tied to the following D-flat in meas. 132) instead of an E-flat. The autograph of Albéniz's orchestration of "El puerto" is located in the Biblioteca de Catalunya. It was to be included in a multimovement work called *1re. Suite d' orchestre*.

3. Fête-Dieu à Séville (F-sharp)

   Date of composition: 1905

   Comment: Dated autograph: Paris, 30 December 1905. Biblioteca del Orfeó Català. In the autograph the title is "No. 3 Seville (La Fête-Dieu)." The Dover edition translates the title to "El Corpus en Sevilla."

2me. Cahier

NOTE: The autograph of the *2me. cahier* preserved at the Biblioteca del Orfeó Català contains the three pieces listed below, but in a different order. In the autograph, "Triana" appears first, as "No. 1," "Almería" is second, and "Rondeña" is third as "No. 3." As described below, the order of these three pieces was changed in the first published edition.

1. Rondeña (D major)

   Date of composition: 1906

   Comment: Dated autograph: Nice, 17 October 1906. Biblioteca del Orfeó Català, in Barcelona.

2. Almería (G major)

   Date of composition: 1906

   Comment: Dated autograph: Paris, 27 June 1906. Biblioteca del Orfeó Català.

3. Triana (F-sharp minor)

Date of composition: 1906

Other editions: Kalmus, 1970?   Albéniz, *Collected Works*, vol. 1
                     Ashley, 1979   Albéniz, *Selected Works for Piano Solo*

Comment: Dated autograph: Paris, 23 January 1906. Biblioteca del Orfeó Català.

3e. Cahier

1. El Albaicín (B-flat minor)

Date of composition: 1906

Comment: Dated autograph: Nice, 4 November 1906. Title in French: "L'Albaicin." Biblioteca de Catalunya, Departament de Música. A wrong note in meas. 175 is repeated in all available editions—the bass line moves from G-flat (meas. 173-74) to F-flat (meas. 174-75) to E-flat (meas. 176-77). In measure 175 there is an A-flat (instead of an F-flat) tied to the F-flat in meas. 176. The autograph however, has the correct note, F-flat.

2. El polo (F minor)

Date of composition: 1906

Comment: Dated autograph: Nice, 16 December 1906. Biblioteca del Orfeó Català.

3. Lavapiés (D-flat major)

Date of composition: 1906

Comment: Dated autograph: Nice, 24 November 1906. Autograph at the Museu de la Música in Barcelona.
        The proofs of the original edition, with corrections made by the composer, are located at the Biblioteca del Orfeó Català.

4e. Cahier

1. Málaga (B-flat minor)

Date of composition: 1907

Comment: Dated autograph: Paris, July 1907. Biblioteca de Catalunya, Departament de Música.

2. Jerez (E major)

Date of composition: 1909

Comment: Dated autograph: Nice, January 1909. Biblioteca de Catalunya, Departament de Música.

3. Eritaña (E-flat major)

Date of composition: 1907

Comment: Dated autograph: Paris, August 1907. Biblioteca de Catalunya, Departament de Música.

48   Yvonne en visite!

No. 1 La Révérence! (A minor)
No. 2 Joyeuse Recontre, et quelques pénibles événemements!! (G major)

No. 1 LA RÉVÉRENCE!

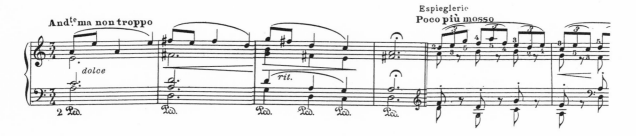

No. 2 JOYEUSE RECONTRE, ET QUELQUES PÉNIBLES ÉVÉNEMEMENTS!!

Date of composition:	before 1909
First edition:	Rouart/Mutuelle 1909
Other editions:	Ricordi, 1973; reprinted, 1986

Plate number: E. 3123. M.

Il mio primo Albéniz — only no. 1, "La Révérence"

Comment: Extracted from *L'Album pour enfants, petits et grands*, a collection of pieces for children including works of other composers.

49   Navarra (A-flat major)

[continued]

49   Navarra — [*continued*]

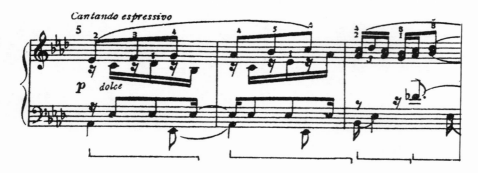

Date of composition: 1909

First edition: Mutuelle, ca. 1910

Other editions: Unión Musical Española, 1912   Reprint of Edition Mutuelle
   Marks, 1938
   Salabert
   International
   Ashley, 1979
   Kalmus, 1970?   Albéniz, *Collected Works*, vol. 1

Comment: Autograph in the Biblioteca de Catalunya, Departament de Música. Score was left unfinished by the composer; the last 24 measures are by Deodat de Sévérac, his pupil.

50   Azulejos

No. 1 Prélude (A major)

Date of composition: 1909

First edition: Rouart, 1911

Other editions: Unión Musical Española, ca. 1912
   Max Eschig, 1930?

Comment: *Azulejos* (tiles) probably meant to be a new series of short pieces or "tiles." Albéniz was able to write only the first piece, "Prélude" before he died. He left it unfinished and it was completed by Enrique Granados about a year after the composer's death, on 25 May 1910. It has not been clearly established how much of the published score was added by Granados.[25]

---

[25] Antonio Iglesias, *Isaac Albéniz: Su obra para piano*, vol. 1 (Madrid: Editorial Alpuerto, 1987), 50-51.

PART 3 APPENDIXES

APPENDIX A

EARLY COMPOSITIONS ALLEGEDLY
WRITTEN BY ALBÉNIZ

The compositions listed below are not included in the main body of this catalog. Unless otherwise stated, these are cited by Gabriel Laplane in his catalog of Albéniz's works.[1] With the exception of *Marcha nupcial* (a work that apparently was published and that Laplane was able to authenticate), Laplane indicates that he knows of these works only as mentioned by Antonio de Guerra y Alarcón.[2] These compositions were presumably written early in Albéniz's career as a composer (before 1889).

1 **Marcha militar,** para piano por el niño de ocho años Isaac Albéniz

Dedicated "al excelentísimo señor Vizconde de Brush." Laplane and Iglesias[3] give Calcografía de B. Eslava, Madrid, as the publisher. This is most likely the earliest recognized composition by Albéniz. Collet mentions it as Albéniz's first published composition.[4]

2 **Burgos,** para piano

This composition is not listed by Laplane; however, it is mentioned by Collet in a quote by Joseph de Marliave.[5]

3 **Dos caprichos para piano**

4 **Dos caprichos Andaluces**

5 **Dos grandes estudios de concierto**

6 **Three Mazurkas**

---

[1] Laplane, 191-92.

[2] Antonio Guerra y Alarcón, *Isaac Albéniz: Notas crítico-biográficas* (Madrid: Escuela tipográfica del Hospicio, 1886). Laplane cites this biography by title only in his bibliography. It is also cited in Henry Collet, *Albéniz et Granados* (Paris: Librairie Félix Alcan, 1926), 13-14. This biography apparently was based on an interview given by Albéniz to Guerra y Alarcón. Unfortunately, it is not very reliable.

[3] Iglesias, 393.

[4] Collet, 36.

[5] Ibid., 105; Joseph de Marliave, "Isaac Albéniz," *Etudes musicales* 6 (1917): 130.

7   Marcha nupcial

8   Pavana española

Mentioned by Iglesias, who speculates that perhaps it might be the same piece as *Pavana*, op. 12, or *Pavana fácil para manos pequeñas*, op. 83, since no details are known about it.[6]

9   Sonata No. 2

10   Sonata No. 6

Albéniz presumably wrote seven sonatas for piano. Three complete sonatas are still extant (nos. 3, 4, and 5) and single movements of two others are also available (nos. 1 and 7). Therefore it can be assumed that Albéniz also composed a second and a sixth sonata, which have been lost.

11   Suite morisca

       Marcha de la caravana
       La noche
       Danza de las esclavas
       Zambra

Suite morisca is also mentioned by Marliave, who is quoted by Collet.[7]

---

[6] Iglesias, 395.

[7] Collet, 105; Marliave, 130.

APPENDIX B

CHRONOLOGICAL OUTLINE OF
ALBÉNIZ'S LIFE AND CAREER

1860 May 29   Isaac Manuel Francisco Albéniz y Pascual was born in Camprodón, the Catalan province of Gerona in northern Spain, near the French border. His father was Ángel Albéniz, from Vitoria, and his mother was Dolores Pascual, from Figueras.[1]

1861   His family moved to Barcelona.

1864   Albéniz gave his first piano recital in Barcelona.

1868   He published his first composition, *Marcha militar*, for piano.

1869   Tour of concerts of Isaac and Clementina, his sister, throughout Catalonia, organized by their father.

1870   Albéniz enrolled at the Escuela Nacional de Música y Declamación (present-day Real Conservatorio de Madrid). His family had moved to Madrid the previous year.

1872   Albéniz was concertizing throughout Spain and was considered a child prodigy. His repertory included works by Scarlatti, Bach, Beethoven, Schumann, and Chopin.

ca. 1873   According to some sources, when Albéniz was thirteen or fourteen years old, he ran away from home and stowed away in a ship bound to Argentina. Apparently, while in Argentina, he led a precarious life supporting himself first by playing in cafés whenever he could, and later performing a series of concerts in Buenos Aires, Uruguay, and Brazil (these concerts were presumably organized by fellow countrymen). According to these sources, he returned to Spain when he became ill with yellow fever.[2] However, there is no evidence of this trip other than what Albéniz related to friends and in interviews. Albéniz kept a detailed diary during his youth, but there are some gaps on it and there is no mention in his album of a trip to South America.

---

[1] Collet, 12.

[2] Raux Deledicque, 126-30.

1874	Blanca Albéniz, Isaac's sister, commited suicide after learning that she was not accepted as a singer in the Teatro de la Zarzuela.

1875   Albéniz traveled to Puerto Rico and Cuba, where he played a series of concerts.

1876 May 2   Albéniz enrolled in the Leipzig Conservatory but stayed there for less than two months. He studied piano with Louis Maas, theory and composition with Carl Piutti, and also briefly with Salomon Jadassohn. Albéniz abandoned his studies at the Leipzig Conservatory on 24 June 1876.[3]

1876 October 17   He was accepted at the Conservatoire Royal de Musique in Brussels where he was to have the longest period of formal instruction, about three years. He took harmony and solfège classes, and studied piano with Brassin. Albéniz finished his studies at the Conservatoire in September 1879, after winning first prize in a piano competition. His studies in Brussels were made under the sponsorship of Alfonso XII, the king of Spain.[4]

1880 August 18   This is the famous date in which the meeting between Albéniz and Franz Liszt allegedly took place in Budapest. However, there are so many conflicts with this date that it is possible to assume that this encounter actually never happened, though there can be no certainty in either case (see Walter Clark's commentary).[5]

1883 June 23   He married Rosina Jordana and settled in Barcelona.

1883   Albéniz began to study composition with Felipe Pedrell, Spanish composer, scholar, and father of the nationalist movement in Spanish music. Pedrell devoted his life to the development of a school inspired by the wealth of Spanish folk song and the rich tradition of early Spanish church and organ music. His influence on Albéniz was significant. Although Albéniz had occasionally used a melodic gesture or rhythm associated with the music of his native land, under Pedrell he systematically began to incorporate elements from Spanish folk music into his compositions.

1884-85   Series of concerts in the south of France and in Paris.

1885   Albéniz and his family moved to Madrid. He taught piano, composed, and performed a great deal.

Alfonso, Albéniz's first child, was born.

1888   Triumphant series of twenty concerts in Paris and Barcelona presented by "Pianos Erard et Cie."

---

[3] Walter Aaron Clark, "Albéniz in Leipzig and Brussels: New Data from Conservatory Records," *Inter-American Music Review* 11 (Fall-Winter 1990): 114-15.

[4] Ibid.

[5] Ibid.

1889-92	Albéniz's career as a concert pianist reached its peak. Tours of concerts in France, Scotland, England, Belgium, Germany, and Austria. Albéniz's virtuosity was highly praised wherever he went.
1889 July 23	Albéniz's second child was born, a daughter named Enriqueta.
1890 April 20	His daughter Laura was born in Barcelona.
1890 to 1893	Albéniz lived in London. He was engaged as principal conductor and composer at the Prince of Wales Theatre. He began to dedicate more time to composition and concentrated on stage works and songs. A long collaboration and friendship began with Francis B. Money-Coutts, a wealthy English lawyer also known as a poet and writer. Money-Coutts wrote some of the librettos for Albéniz's stage works and supplied the composer with a steady income throughout his life (and a pension to his widow after Albéniz's death), playing in fact the customary role of a patron.[6]
1893	His comic opera *The Magic Opal* is premièred at the Lyric Theatre in London on January 19. The libretto was by Arthur Law. A revised version of *The Magic Opal*, renamed *The Magic Ring*, was presented at the Lyric Teatre on April 11.[7]
1893 to 1894	Albéniz lived in Madrid.
1894	Production of his zarzuela *San Antonio de la Florida*, with a libretto by Eusebio Sierra, at Teatro de Apolo, Madrid, on October 26. Also *La Sortija*, a translation to Spanish of *The Magic Opal* by Sierra, is premièred on November 23 at the Teatro de la Zarzuela, Madrid.
1894	Albéniz moved with his family to Paris. He became in close contact with French musicians from the Schola Cantorum, particularly Gabriel Fauré, Charles Bordes, and Ernest Chausson, and began studies of counterpoint with Vincent d'Indy.[8] He was an avid listener in the concerts of the Société Nationale de Musique, and rapidly began to absorb the sophisticated compositional techniques of his French colleagues. His relocation to Paris proved to be a decisive turning point in his development as a composer.
1895 May 8	Only production of his opera *Henry Clifford*, libretto by Francis Money-Coutts, at the Gran Teatro del Liceo, in Barcelona.
1896 January 5	First production of his lyric comedy *Pepita Jiménez*, the most successful of Albéniz's stage works, at the Liceo in Barcelona. It was based on a novel by Juan Valera with a libretto

---

[6] Walter Aaron Clark, "Isaac Albéniz's Faustian Pact: A Study in Patronage," *Musical Quarterly* 76 (1992): 469-80.

[7] Ibid., 468.

[8] Ibid., 472.

1896 — [*continued*]	by Francis Money-Coutts. *Pepita Jiménez* was considered a valuable addition to the school of Spanish national opera. It was also successfully presented in Prague (1897), and Brussels (1905) during the composer's lifetime.[9]
1897	Albéniz was appointed substitute professor of piano at the Schola Cantorum in Paris. This was an excellent position for Albéniz, who taught classes of interpretation to serious, advanced music students.[10] He was at the Schola until 1899, when he was forced to give up his position due to health problems.[11]
1898	Albéniz made a trip to Granada (in the Andalusian region of Spain), site of the palace and citadel of the "Alhambra," one of the most celebrated monuments left by the Moors in Spain. The trip inspired his composition for piano "La Vega" (from *The Alhambra*) and most likely "El Albaicín" (from *Iberia*). Albaicín is the gypsy quarter in Granada.
1900	Albéniz's mother died.
1900-02	He returned to Spain, stayed first in Barcelona and later in Madrid.
1902	Albéniz moved back to Paris.
1903	He moved again, now to Nice. Albéniz's father died.
1906	First performance of the first book of *Iberia* by Blanche Selva, who will première each one of the three remaining books shortly after their composition.[12]
1909 May 18	Albéniz died in Cambô-les-Bains, France, after an extended battle with Bright's disease (a kidney disorder). He was eleven days short of his 49th birthday.

---

[9] Clark, 473, 485.

[10] Raux Deledicque, 126-30.

[11] Clark, 477.

[12] Iglesias, 378.

APPENDIX C

COLLECTIONS OF ALBÉNIZ PIANO WORKS
[Titles within square brackets correspond to the titles used in the present catalog]

Albéniz, *Selected Works for Piano Solo*

Ashley Publications (1979)   Carlstadt, NJ 07072

Arabe [*Serenata árabe*]
Barcarolle catalane [op. 23]
Cadiz-gaditana
Cotillon Waltz [*Cotillon (Carte blanche)*, vals de salón]
Champagne Waltz [*Cotillon (Carte blanche)*, vals de salón or Champagne, vals]
Espagne [*Espagne: Souvenirs*, no. 2, "Asturies"]
Estudio impromptu [op. 56]
Gavotta [*3e Suite ancienne*, no. 2, "Gavotte"]
Mallorca [*Mallorca: Barcarolle*, op. 202]
Minuetto [*3e Suite ancienne*, no. 1, "Minuetto"]
Navarra
Rapsodia cubana [op. 66]
Sérénade espagnole [*Serenata española*, op. 181]
Six Little Waltzes, op. 25 [*Seis pequeños valses*, op. 25]
Songs of Spain [*Chants d'Espagne*, op. 232]
Torre Bermeja [*Douze Pièces caractéristiques pour piano*, op. 92, no. 12]
Triana [*Iberia*, 2e. cahier]
Zambra granadina [*Zambra granadina: Danse orientale*]

Spanish Sketchbook for the Piano

Boston Music Co. (1921)   Boston, MA 02116

Alborada [*Recuerdos de viaje*, op. 71, no. 3, "Alborada"]
Canción [*Recuerdos de viaje*, op. 71, no. 7, "En la playa"]
Danza [*Seis danzas españolas*, no. 4]
En la Alhambra [*Recuerdos de viaje*, op. 71, no. 4]
Habanera [*Seis danzas españolas*, no. 1]
Malagueña [*Recuerdos de viaje*, op. 71, no. 6, "Rumores de la Caleta: Malagueña"]
Recuerdo [*Seis danzas españolas*, no. 5]
Serenata Andaluza [*Seis danzas españolas*, no. 3]

Albéniz, *Iberia and España:*
Two Complete Works for Solo Piano

Dover Publications (1987)   Mineola, NY 11501

> España: 6 Hojas de album, op. 165
> Iberia: 12 nouvelles "impressions" en quatre cahiers

Albéniz, *Trois Nouvelles Compositions pour piano*

C. Ducci & Co. (1890)

> Cadiz-gaditana
> Sérénade espagnole [*Serenata española*, op. 181]
> Zambra granadina

Collected Works of Isaac Albéniz for Piano Solo

Kalmus Piano Series (ca. 1970)   Belwin Mills, Melville, NY 11746

Vol. 1

> Célèbre Sérénade espagnole [*Serenata española*, op. 181] (published also in vol. 2)
> Espagne: Souvenirs, no. 2, "Asturies"
> Mallorca: Barcarola, op. 202
> Navarra
> Serenata árabe
> Triana [*Iberia*, 2e. Cahier]
> Zambra granadina: Danse orientale

Vol. 2

> Arabe [*Serenata árabe*]
> Barcarolle catalane [op. 23]
> Cadiz-gaditana
> Estudio impromptu [op. 56]
> Gavotta (*Suite ancienne*, no. 3)
> Rapsodia cubana, op. 66
> Serenade espagnole
> Torre Bermeja: Serenata, Piezas características, op. 92, no. 12 [*Douze Pièces caractéristiques*, op. 92]
> Troisième Suite ancienne, no. 1, "Minuetto"
> Troisième Suite ancienne, no. 2, "Gavotta"

Albéniz, *Dix Pièces*, piano original

Alphonse Leduc (1922)   Paris, France

> Aragonaise: Jota espagnole [*Deux Danses espagnoles*, op. 164, no. 1]
> L'Automne, Les Saisons [*Album of Miniatures (Les Saisons)*, op. 101, no. 3, "L'Automne"]

Berceuse, Rêves, op. 201 [*Rêves*, op. 201, no. 1, "Berceuse"]
Chant d'amour, Rêves, op. 201 [*Rêves*, op. 201, no. 3, "Chant d'amour"]
L'Été, Les Saisons [*Album of Miniatures (Les Saisons)*, op. 101, no. 2, "L'Été"]
L'Hiver, Les Saisons [*Album of Miniatures (Les Saisons)*, op. 101, no. 4, "L'Hiver"]
Menuet
Le Printemps, Les Saisons [*Album of Miniatures (Les Saisons)*, op. 101, no. 1, "Le Printemps"]
Scherzino, Rêves, op. 201 [*Rêves*, op. 201, no. 2, "Scherzino"]
Tango espagnol [*Deux Danses espagnoles*, op. 164, no. 2]

Il mio primo Albéniz

Ricordi & C. Editori (1973, 1986)   Milan, Italy

Capriccio catalano [*España*, op. 165, no. 5, "Serenata"]
La riverenza! [*Yvonne en visite*, no. 1, "La Révérence!"]
Pavana (per piccole mani), op. 83 [*Pavana fácil para manos pequeñas*]
Preludio [*España*, op. 165, no. 1, "Prélude"]
Valzer in la bemolle maggiore [*Seis pequeños valses*, op. 25, no. 2]
Valzer in mi bemolle maggiore [*Seis pequeños valses*, op. 25, no. 6]

APPENDIX D

SELECTED LIST OF COMPOSITIONS FOR PIANO BY ALBÉNIZ
GRADED ACCORDING TO LEVEL OF DIFFICULTY

Composition	*Publisher*

INTERMEDIATE LEVEL

Pavana-capricho, op. 12 — Unión Musical Española (UME)

Seis pequeños valses, op. 25 — UME, Kalmus

Pavana fácil para manos pequeñas, op. 83 — UME, Ricordi

España: Six Feuilles d'album, op. 165 — UME, Schott, Carl Fisher, Dover, Peters
- No. 1 Prélude
- No. 2 Tango
- No. 3 Malagueña
- No. 4 Serenata
- No. 5 Capricho catalán
- No. 6 Zortzico

Yvonne en visite — Rouart, Ricordi (*Il mio primo Albéniz*, no. 2, only)
- No. 1 La Révérerence!
- No. 2 Joyeuse Recontre, et quelques pénibles événements!!

MEDIUM DIFFICULTY

Suite española, op. 47 — UME, Salabert, Schott, Kalmus, International
- No. 1 Granada: Serenata
- No. 2 Cataluña: Curranda
- No. 3 Sevilla: Sevillanas
- No. 4 Cadiz: Canción
- No. 5 Asturias: Leyenda
- No. 6 Aragón: Fantasía
- No. 7 Castillas: Seguidillas
- No. 8 Cuba: Capricho

Recuerdos de viaje, op. 71   UME, Ashley, International
     No. 1 En el mar
     No. 2 Leyenda: Barcarola
     No. 3 Alborada
     No. 4 En la Alhambra
     No. 5 Puerta de tierra: Bolero
     No. 6 Rumores de la Caleta: Malagueña
     No. 7 En la playa

Douze Pièces caractéristiques pour piano, op. 92   UME, Kalmus, Ashley
     No.   3 Barcarolle: Ciel sans nuage
     No. 12 Torre Bermeja: Serenata

Serenata española, op. 181   UME, Kalmus (*Collected Works*, vol. 2)

Mallorca: Barcarola, op. 202   UME, Salabert, Kalmus (*Collected Works*, vol. 1)

Zambra granadina: Danse orientale   UME, Ashley, Kalmus (*Collected Works*, vol. 1)

Chants d'Espagne, op. 232   UME, Kalmus, International
     No. 1 Prélude
     No. 2 Orientale
     No. 3 Sous les palmier: Danse espagnole
     No. 4 Córdoba
     No. 5 Seguidillas

España: Souvenirs   UME, Ashley, Kalmus (*Collected Works*, vol. 1)
     No. 2 Asturies

Iberia (1er. Cahier)   UME, Kalmus, Dover
     1. Evocación
     2. El puerto

DIFFICULT

Barcarola, op. 23   UME, Ashley, Kalmus (*Collected Works*, vol. 2), Salabert

Deseo: Estudio de concierto, op. 40   UME, Kalmus

España: Souvenirs   UME
     No. 1 Prélude

Estudio impromptu, op. 56   UME, Kalmus, Ashley

The Alhambra: Suite pour le piano
    No. 1 La Vega

UME, Kalmus

Iberia: 12 nouvelles "impressions" en quatre cahiers
    1er. Cahier
        3. Fête-Dieu à Séville
    2e. Cahier
        1. Rondeña
        2. Almería
        3. Triana
    3e. Cahier
        1. El Albaicín
        2. El polo
        3. Lavapiés
    4e. Cahier
        1. Málaga
        2. Jerez
        3. Eritaña

Dover, UME, Salabert, Kalmus, International, Marks. (The Dover edition contains all four books of *Iberia* in one volume, plus *España*, op. 165.)

Navarra

UME, Salabert, International Kalmus (*Collected Works*, vol. 1), Marks

APPENDIX E

DISCOGRAPHY

Some of the recordings listed in this appendix are not commercially available any longer. However, a great number of them can be found in the Library of Congress and other libraries across the country.

The number at the left side of the title of each composition corresponds to the number given to each piece in the main body of the catalog of Albéniz's piano works.

1 Pavana-capricho, op. 12 (E minor)

Alicia de Larrocha   *Spanish Encores*, London: Decca CS 6953, 1974
Rena Kiriakou   *Albéniz Piano Music*, vol. 1, 3-Vox SVBX-5403

7 Suite española, op. 47

No. 1 Granada: Serenata (F major)
No. 2 Cataluña: Curranda (G minor)
No. 3 Sevilla: Sevillanas (G major)
No. 4 Cadiz: Canción (D-flat major)
No. 5 Asturias: Leyenda (G minor)
No. 6 Aragón: Fantasía (F major)
No. 7 Castillas: Seguidillas (F-sharp major)
No. 8 Cuba: Capricho (E-flat major)

Alicia de Larrocha   London: CD Decca 417887-2, 1987
Ricardo Requejo   France: Claves DC 50-8003/4, 1986
Gonzalo Soriano   Boston Records, B 302, 195-?

Individual pieces

No. 1 Granada: Serenata

Ruth Laredo   CD MCA Classics MCAD-6265

No. 3 Sevilla: Sevillanas

Rafael Arroyo   France: Adès CD 13207-2, 1973
Gérard Gahnassia   Pianissime MAG-2018
José Iturbi   *Spanish Piano Music*, Angel 35628

Beatriz Klien	Turnabout TV 34327, 1970
Ruth Laredo	CD MCA Classics MCAD-6265
Alicia de Larrocha	*Spanish Encores*, London: Decca CS 6953, 1974
Leonard Pennario	Capitol 8190

No. 4 Cadiz: Canción. See also *Serenata española*, op. 181

Gérard Gahnassia	Pianissime MAG-2018
Beatriz Klien	Turnabout TV 34327, 1970
Ruth Laredo	CD MCA Classics MCAD-6265

No. 5 Asturias: Leyenda

Arroyo	Decca 17396
Jorge Bolet	Boston 300
Gérard Gahnassia	Pianissime MAG-2018
José Iturbi	*Spanish Piano Music*, Angel 35628

No. 6 Aragón: Fantasía

Ruth Laredo	CD MCA Classics MCAD-6265

No. 8 Cuba: Capricho

Gérard Gahnassia	Pianissime MAG-2018

11   Siete estudios en los tonos naturales mayores, op. 65

No. 1 (C major)
No. 2 (G major)
No. 3 (D major)
No. 4 (A major)
No. 5 (E major)
No. 6 (B major)
No. 7 (F major)

Rena Kiriakou	*Albéniz Piano Music*, vol. 1, 3-Vox SVBX-5403

14   3ª [i.e., Tercera] Sonata, op. 68 (A-flat major)

Allegretto
Andante
Allegro assai

Rena Kiriakou	*Albéniz Piano Music*, vol. 1, 3-Vox SVBX-5403

17   Rapsodia española, piano seul, op. 70 (D minor)

This work has been recorded only in the piano and orchestra version: Alicia de Larrocha with Frühbeck de Burgos and the London Philharmonic, London 410289-2 LH.

18　Recuerdos de viaje, op. 71

　　　No. 1 En el mar (A-flat major)
　　　No. 2 Leyenda: Barcarola (E-flat major)
　　　No. 3 Alborada (A major)
　　　No. 4 En la Alhambra (A minor)
　　　No. 5 Puerta de tierra: Bolero (D major)
　　　No. 6 Rumores de la caleta: Malagueña (D minor)
　　　No. 7 En la playa (A-flat major)

　　　　Rena Kiriakou　　　　　*Albéniz Piano Music*, vol. 1, 3-Vox SVBX-5403

Individual movements

No. 5 Puerta de tierra: Bolero

　　　　Alicia de Larrocha　　　*Spanish Encores*, London: Decca CS 6953, 1974

No. 6 Rumores de la caleta: Malagueña

　　　　Alfred Cortot　　　　　*The Art of Alfred Cortot*, Seraphim 60143, 1970 (recorded June 1930)
　　　　José Iturbi　　　　　　France: RCA 630.339, 1967
　　　　Beatriz Klien　　　　　Turnabout TV 34237, 1970
　　　　Alicia de Larrocha　　　*Spanish Encores*, London: Decca CS 6953, 1974

29　Douze Pièces caractéristiques pour piano, op. 92

　　　No. 1 Gavotte (G major)
　　　No. 2 Minuetto a Sylvia (A major)
　　　No. 3 Barcarolle: Ciel sans nuage (E-flat major)
　　　No. 4 Prière (E-flat major)
　　　No. 5 Conchita: Polka (F major)
　　　No. 6 Pilar: Valse (A major)
　　　No. 7 Zambra (G minor)
　　　No. 8 Pavana (F minor)
　　　No. 9 Polonesa (E-flat major)
　　　No. 10 Mazurka (G minor)
　　　No. 11 Staccato: Capricho (A major)
　　　No. 12 Torre Bermeja: Serenata (E major)

　　　　No recording of the complete work.

Individual movements

No. 12 Torre Bermeja: Serenata

　　　　Frank Marshall　　　　　Columbia ML 4294

32　Seconde Suite espagnole

　　　No. 1 Zaragoza: Capricho (E-flat major)
　　　No. 2 Sevilla (D major)

　　　　No recording of the complete work.

No. 1 Zaragoza: Capricho

     Alicia de Larrocha   Musical Heritage Society MHS 1571, 1973

36   **Deux Dances [*sic*] espagnoles**, op. 164

    No. 1 Aragón: Jota aragonesa (E-flat major) (see also *Suite española*, op. 47, no. 6, "Jota")
    No. 2 Tango (A minor)

     Eileen Joyce   Decca DL 9528 (only no. 2, "Tango")

37   **España: Six Feuilles d'album**, op. 165

    No. 1 Prélude (D minor)
    No. 2 Tango (D major)
    No. 3 Malagueña (E minor/B Phrygian)
    No. 4 Serenata (G minor)
    No. 5 Capricho catalán (E-flat major)
    No. 6 Zortzico (E major)

     Pierre Huybregts   Centaur CD CR-2026, 1989

Individual movements

No. 2 Tango

Rafael Arroyo	France: Adès CD 13207-2, 1973
Leonid Brumberg	Soviet Union: Melodia C10 05795-6, 1970
José Iturbi	*Spanish Piano Music*, Angel 35628
Beatriz Klien	Turnabout TV 34327, 1970
Alicia de Larrocha	*Spanish Encores*, London: Decca CS 6953, 1974

No. 3 Malagueña

     Alicia de Larrocha   *Spanish Encores*, London: Decca CS 6953, 1974

39   **Serenata española**, op. 181 (see *Suite española*, op. 47, no. 4, "Cadiz," same composition)

Santiago Rodriguez	*Santiago Rodriguez Plays Ginastera*, Elan 2202, 1986
José Iturbi	*Spanish Piano Music*, Angel 35628

40   **Rêves**, op. 201

    No. 1 Berceuse (G major)
    No. 2 Scherzino (C major)
    No. 3 Chant d'amour (A major)

     Rena Kiriakou   *Albéniz Piano Music*, vol. 1, 3-Vox SVBX-5403

41   **Mallorca: Barcarola**, op. 202 (F-sharp minor)

Rafael Arroyo	Decca 91151
Gérard Gahnassia	Pianissime MAG-2018

Rena Kiriakou	*Albéniz Piano Music*, vol. 1, 3-Vox SVBX-5403
Alicia de Larrocha	Musical Heritage Society MHS 1571, 1973
Santiago Rodriguez	*Santiago Rodriguez Plays Ginastera*, Elan 2202, 1986

42   Zambra granadina: Danse orientale (D minor)

Alicia de Larrocha	Musical Heritage Society MHS 1571, 1973

44   Chants d'Espagne, op. 232

No. 1 Prélude (G minor)
No. 2 Orientale (D minor)
No. 3 Sous les palmier, danse espagnole (E-flat major)
No. 4 Córdoba (D minor)
No. 5 Seguidillas (F-sharp major)

José Achániz	Westminster 2217 (2 records)
Ruth Laredo	CD MCA Classics MCAD-6265
Alicia de Larrocha	London: Decca CSA 2235, 1973
Orazio Frugoni	Vox 9420 (except for no. 2, "Orientale")
Leonard Pennario	Capitol P 8319, 1956?
Ricardo Requejo	France: Claves CD 50-8003/4, 1986
Gustavo Romero	CD REM 311150, 1990

Individual movements

No. 1 Prélude

Jorge Bolet	Boston 300
Frank Marshall	Columbia ML 4294
Marisa Regules	Esoteric 3002 USA

No. 3 Sous les palmier: Dance espagnole

Alfred Cortot	Everest Records, Archive of Piano Music 906

The title of this composition is erroneously listed as "Under the Palms, from 'Dance Espagnole,' op. 56, no. 1."

No. 4 Córdoba

Rafael Arroyo	France: Adès CD 13207-2, 1973
Jorge Bolet	Boston 300
Leonid Brumberg	Soviet Union: Melodia C10 05795-6, 1970
Jorge Copeland	MGM E 187 & E 3025
Amparo Iturbi	France: Victor LM 1788 and RCA A-630231
José Iturbi	*Spanish Piano Music*, Angel 35628
Beatriz Klien	Turnabout TV 34327, 1970
Menahem Pressler	MGM E 3129
Marisa Regules	USA: Esoteric 3002

No. 5 Seguidillas

Alfred Cortot	*The Art of Alfred Cortot*, Seraphim 60143, 1970 (recorded June 1930)
Marisa Regules	Esoteric 3002 USA
Paolo Spagnolo	London: Decca LLP 1040

46   The Alhambra: Suite pour le piano

No. 1 La Vega (A-flat major)

Alicia de Larrocha	Musical Heritage Society MHS 1571, 1973
Alicia de Larrocha	Hispavox HH 10 86-87

47   Iberia: 12 nouvelles "impressions" en quatre cahiers

1er. cahier
1. Evocación (A-flat minor)
2. El puerto (D-flat major)
3. Fête-Dieu à Séville (F-sharp minor)

2e. cahier
1. Rondeña (D major)
2. Almería (G major)
3. Triana (F-sharp minor)

3e. cahier
1. El Albaicín (B-flat minor)
2. El polo (F minor)
3. Lavapiés (D-flat major)

4e. cahier
1. Málaga (B-flat minor)
2. Jerez (A minor/E Phrygian)
3. Eritaña (E-flat major)

Aybar	Connoisseur 2601
Block	2-Connoisseur 2120-1, also EMI 167-053.330/1
Aldo Ciccolini	2-Seraphim S-60
José Echániz	Westminster WAL 2217
José Falgarona	Vox 9212
Rena Kiriakou	*Albéniz Piano Music*, vol. 1, 3-Vox SVBX-5403
Irene Kohler	England: Concert Artist LPA 1015-16
Alicia de Larrocha	Columbia M2L 268, 1956; recorded in Spain by Hispavox
Alicia de Larrocha	London: Decca CD 417887-2, 1987
Alicia de Larrocha	London: Decca CSA 2235, 1973
Leopoldo Querol	London: Ducretet-Thompson DTL 93022-3, 1954?
Ricardo Requejo	France: Claves CD 50-8003/4, 1986
Blanca Uribe	2-Orion ORS 75202-3, 1976

Individual movements

Evocación

Claudio Arrau	Columbia ML 4194
Michel Bourgeot	Coronet 3003

| Yvonne Loriod | France: Adès ACD 14071-2, 1957-85 |
| Benita Meshulam | Classic Masters CMCD-1033 |

El puerto

Claudio Arrau	Columbia ML 4194
Michel Bourgeot	Coronet 3003
Benita Meshulam	Classic Masters CMCD-1033

Fête-Dieu à Séville

Claudio Arrau	Columbia ML 4194
Rafael Arroyo	London/USA: Decca TW 91151
Michel Bourgeot	Coronet 3003
Yvonne Loriod	France: Adès ACD 14071-2, 1957-85
Benita Meshulam	Classic Masters CMCD-1033

Rondeña

Claudio Arrau	Columbia ML 4194
Rafael Arroyo	London/USA: Decca TW 91151
Benita Meshulam	Classic Masters CMCD-1033

Almería

Claudio Arrau	Columbia ML 4194
Yvonne Loriod	France: Adès ACD 14071-2, 1957-85
Benita Meshulam	Classic Masters CMCD-1033

Triana

Claudio Arrau	Columbia ML 4194
Leonid Brumberg	Soviet Union: Melodia C10 05795-6, 1970
Beatriz Klien	Turnabout TV 34327, 1970
Yvonne Loriod	France: Adès ACD 14071-2, 1957-85
Benita Meshulam	Classic Masters CMCD-1033
Abbey Simon	*The Piano Virtuoso*, Turnabout 34783

El Albaicín

Rafael Arroyo	London/USA: Decca TW 91151
Yvonne Loriod	France: Adès ACD 14071-2, 1957-85
Benita Meshulam	Classic Masters CMCD-1033

El polo

| Yvonne Loriod | France: Adès ACD 14071-2, 1957-85 |

Málaga

| Benita Meshulam | Classic Masters CMCD-1033 |

Jerez

    Yvonne Loriod   France: Adès ACD 14071-2, 1957-85

Eritaña

    Yvonne Loriod   France: Adès ACD 14071-2, 1957-85

49   Navarra (A-flat major)

Joaquín Achucarro	RCA RL-31404
Leonid Brumberg	Soviet Union: Melodia C10 05795-6, 1970
José Echániz	Westminster 2217
Alicia de Larrocha	London: Decca CSA 2235, 1973
Alicia de Larrocha	London: Decca CD 417889-2, 1987
Emilio Osta	France: Pacific LDA D 148
Leopoldo Querol	USA: Ducretet DTL 93022-3
Artur Rubinstein	RCA CD 5670-2, 1989 (recorded live, 1961)

50   Azulejos

Alicia de Larrocha	Musical Heritage Society MHS 1571, 1973
Alicia de Larrocha	Hispavox CH 249-10-86

BIBLIOGRAPHY

Albéniz, Isaac. *Impresiones y diarios de viaje.* Ed. Enrique Franco. Madrid: Fundación Isaac Albéniz, 1990.

Arteaga y Pereira, G. *Celebridades musicales.* Barcelona: Centro Editorial Artístico, 1886.

Aviñoa, Xosé. *Conocer y reconocer la música de Albéniz.* México City: Ediciones Daimon de México, 1986.

Chase, Gilbert. *The Music of Spain.* 2nd rev. ed. New York: Dover, 1959.

Clark, Walter Aaron. "Albéniz in Leipzig and Brussels: New Data from Conservatory Records." *Inter-American Music Review* 11 (Fall-Winter 1990): 113-16.

_____. "Isaac Albéniz's Faustian Pact: A Study in Patronage." *Musical Quarterly* 76/4 (1992): 465-87.

_____. "Spanish Music with a Universal Accent: Isaac Albéniz's Opera *Pepita Jiménez.*" Ph.D. dissertation, University of California, Los Angeles, 1992.

Collet, Henry. *Albéniz et Granados.* Paris: Librairie Felix Alcan, 1926.

_____. "Albéniz y Joaquim Malats." *Revista musical catalana* 6 (1909): 377-79.

_____. "Isaac Albéniz." *L'Essor de la musique espagnole au XX siècle,* 50-57. Paris: Édition Max Eschig, 1929.

Dolmenech, Español. "Isaac Albéniz." *Revista de música* [Buenos Aires] 2 (1928): 150-55.

Dumesnil, Maurice. "Prolific Albéniz." *Etude* 67 (1949): 408.

Enciclopedia della musica (1963). S.v. "Zapateado," "Polo."

Fernández Arbós, Enrique. *Arbós* [memorias de]. Madrid: Ediciones Cid, 1963.

Franco, Enrique. "La Suite 'Iberia' di Albéniz." *Nuova rivista musicale italiana* 7/1 (January-March 1973): 51-74.

_____, ed. *Albéniz y su tiempo.* Madrid: Fundación Isaac Albéniz, 1990.

_____, ed. *Imágenes de Isaac Albéniz.* Madrid: Fundación Isaac Albéniz, 1988.

_____, ed. *Isaac Albéniz: Impresiones y diarios de viaje.* Madrid: Fundación Isaac Albéniz, 1990.

Gillespie, John. *Five Centuries of Keyboard Music.* Belmont, Cal.: Wadsworth, 1965; reprint, New York: Dover, 1972.

Gew, Sydney. "The Music for Pianoforte of Albéniz." *Chesterian* 6/42 (1924): 43-48.

Guerra y Alarcón, Antonio. *Isaac Albéniz: Notas crítico-biográficas de tan eminente pianista.* Madrid: Escuela tipográfica del hospicio, 1886; reprint, Madrid: Fundación Isaac Albéniz, 1990.

Heras, Antonio de las. *Vida de Albéniz*. Barcelona: Ediciones Patria, 1940.

Iglesias Antonio. *Isaac Albéniz: Su obra para piano*. 2 vols. Madrid: Editorial Alpuerto, 1987.

Jankélévitch, Vladimir. "Albéniz et l' état de verve." *La Rhapsodie: Verve et improvisation musicale*, 150-79. Paris: Flammarion, Bibliothèque d'Esthétique, 1955.

Jean-Aubry, George. "Isaac Albéniz (1860-1909)." *Musical Times* 58 (December 1917): 535-38.

Kalfa, Jacqueline. "Isaac Albéniz à Paris," *Revue internationale de musique française* 9 (June 1988): 19-37.

Laplane, Gabriel. *Albéniz: Sa vie, son oeuvre*. Préface de Francis Poulenc. Geneva: Editions du Milieu du Monde, 1956. Spanish translation by Bernabé Herrero and Alberto de Michelena, Barcelona: Editorial Noguer, 1958.

Livermore, Ann. *A Short History of Spanish Music*. New York: Vienna House, 1972.

Llorens Cisteró, José María. "El 'lied' en la obra musical de Isaac Albéniz." *Anuario musical* 15 (1960): 123-40.

_____. "Notas inéditas sobre el virtuosismo de Isaac Albéniz y su producción pianística." *Anuario musical* 14 (1959): 91-113.

Marliave, Joseph de. "Isaac Albéniz." *Etudes musicales* 6 (1917): 119-38.

Mast, Paul Buck. "Style and Structure in 'Iberia' by Isaac Albéniz." Ph.D. dissertation, Eastman School of Music, University of Rochester, 1974.

Minor, Martha Danielson. "Hispanic Influences on the Works of French Composers of the Nineteenth and Twentieth Centuries." Ph.D. dissertation, University of Kansas, 1983.

Mitjana, Rafael. "Merlin." *Albéniz y su tiempo*. Madrid: Fundación Isaac Albéniz, 1990.

Montero Alonso, José. *Albéniz: España en "suite."* Barcelona: G. Monterreina, 1988.

The New Grove Dictionary of Music and Musicians (1980). S.v. "Isaac Albéniz," by Tomas Marco; "Fandango"; "Flamenco."

Newman, Ernest. "Music and Musicians: Albéniz and His 'Merlin'." *New Witness* 10 (20 December 1917): 495-96.

Pedrell, Felipe. "Isaac Albéniz, l'home, l'artista y l'obra." *Revista musical catalana*, June 1909, 180-85.

Powell, Linton E. *A History of Spanish Piano Music*. Bloomington: Indiana University Press, 1980.

Raux Deledicque, Miguel. *Albéniz: Su vida inquieta y ardorosa*. Buenos Aires: Ediciones Peuser, 1950.

Romero, A. "A Master Lesson on Asturias from Albéniz's Suite española." *Clavier* 21 (1982): 22-29.

Ruiz Tarazona, Andrés. *Isaac Albéniz, España soñada*. Madrid: Real Musical Editores, 1975.

Salazar, Adolfo. "Isaac Albéniz." *La música contemporanea en España*, 117-53. Madrid: Ediciones La Nave, 1930.

Saperas, Miquel. *Cinc compositors catalans*. Barcelona: Josep Porter, 1975.

Schonberg, Harold C. *The Great Pianists*. New York: Simon and Schuster, 1963.

_____. "Isaac Albéniz, a Runaway Genius." *New York Times*, 11 December 1960.

Seifert, W. "In Memoriam." *Musica* 13 (3 June 1959): 402.

Serra Crespo, José. *Senderos espirituales de Albéniz y Debussy*. Mexico: Costa Amic Editor, 1944.

Soperas Ibañez, Federico. "Isaac Albéniz." *Dos años de música en Europa*, 87-92. Madrid: Espasa-Calpe, 1942.

Torres, Jacinto. "La producción escénica de Isaac Albéniz." *Revista de musicología* 14 (Enero-Septiembre 1991): 167-211.

Tricás Preckler, Mercedes. *Cartas de Paul Dukas a Laura Albéniz*. Bellaterra: Universidad Autónoma de Barcelona, 1983.

Vallas, Léon. *The Theories of Claude Debussy*. Transl. Marie O'Brien. London: Oxford University Press, 1929.

Van Loo, E. "La Vie picaresque d'Isaac Albéniz." *Musica* (Chaix) 67 (October 1959): 35-38.

Van Vechten, Carl. "Isaac Albéniz." *Excavations*, 230-54. New York: Alfred A. Knopf, 1926.

Villalba Muñoz, Luis. "Isaac Albéniz." *Ultimos músicos españoles del siglo XIX*, 161-85. Madrid: I. Alier, 1914.

Villar, Rogelio. "Isaac Albéniz." *Músicos españoles*, 73-79. Madrid: Ediciones "Mateu," 1918.

INDEX

[Page numbers of main entries of compositions use boldface type]

About the Author

Pola Baytelman was born in Santiago, Chile, where she attended the University of Chile's National Conservatory. The recipient of a Fulbright grant to study in the United States, she received the degrees of Master of Music and Artist Diploma from the New England Conservatory, and a Doctor of Musical Arts from the University of Texas at Austin. Pola Baytelman made her debut as a piano soloist with the Chilean Symphony Orchestra at the age of 17 and has since played with numerous orchestras, including the Chilean Philharmonic and the Boston Pops. She has performed extensively in Chile and throughout the United States, including featured television appearances in both countries. Baytelman has presented many performances and lectures on the piano music of Isaac Albéniz. She is presently artist-in-residence at Skidmore College, Saratoga Springs, New York.